LANGUAGE AND L

Dorothy S. Stricklan
Celia Genishi and Donna E.
ADVISORY BOARD: *Richard Allington, Kath*
Anne Haas Dyson, Carole Edelsky, Mary Juzwik,

continued

For volumes in the NCRLL Collection (edited by JoBeth Allen and Donna E. Alvermann) and the Practitioners Bookshelf Series (edited by Celia Genishi and Donna E. Alvermann), as well as other titles in this series, please visit www.tcpress.com.

Choice and Agency
in the
Writing Workshop

Developing Engaged Writers, Grades 4–6

FRED L. HAMEL
FOREWORD BY ANNE HAAS DYSON

TEACHERS COLLEGE PRESS
TEACHERS COLLEGE | COLUMBIA UNIVERSITY
NEW YORK AND LONDON

NATIONAL WRITING PROJECT

Published by Teachers College Press, 1234 Amsterdam Avenue, New York, NY 10027 and National Writing Project, 2105 Bancroft Way, Berkeley, CA 94720-1042.

Through its mission, the National Writing Project (NWP) focuses the knowledge, expertise, and leadership of our nation's educators on sustained efforts to help youth become successful writers and learners. NWP works in partnership with local Writing Project sites, located on nearly 200 university and college campuses, to provide high-quality professional development in schools, universities, libraries, museums, and after-school programs. NWP envisions a future where every person is an accomplished writer, engaged learner, and active participant in a digital, interconnected world.

Cover design by Patricia Palao.

Library of Congress Cataloging-in-Publication Data is available at loc.gov

ISBN 978-0-8077-5855-7 (paper)
ISBN 978-0-8077-7586-8 (ebook)

Printed on acid-free paper
Manufactured in the United States of America

24 23 22 21 20 19 18 17   8 7 6 5 4 3 2 1

To Trinka, with gratitude

The teacher should encounter the child—every child—with humanity and a little awe.
(Ayers, 1998)

The question is whether we can begin to think . . . not in terms of needs we already know but in terms of diversities whose connections we do not yet know.
(May, 2005)

Contents

Foreword

What dangerous activity . . . teaching is. All this plastering on of foreign stuff. Why plaster on at all when there's so much inside already. . . . If only I could get it out and use it as working material.

—Sylvia Ashton-Warner (1963)

As I followed Fred Hamel into Mr. Allegro's lively 4th-grade classroom, I kept thinking of a beloved old book, Sylvia Ashton-Warner's *Teacher* (1963). Her account of her teaching is focused on younger children in a sociopolitically different time and place—children in a Maori village. And it is dated: Ashton-Warner was Eurocentric, aiming to help her students cross the cultural bridge to the academic motherland. Still, that book offered teaching insights that I hear in Hamel's engaging book as well. He does not build in any way on Ashton-Warner, but similar structural forces and everyday emotions compel them both—an affectionate respect for children, an appreciation for the written word, saturated as it can be with the dynamics of children's lives, and a healthy resistance to curricular marching orders from folks who don't know the children in one's class at all.

That opening quote is a case in point. We as teachers have no choice but to build with what the children already know. And what they know, as Hamel describes, is a diversity of semiotic tools—drawing, storytelling, dramatizing, popular media texts and games, appropriated knowledge about all manner of human experiences and yes, if sometimes tentatively, the process and conventions of written language. How they draw on those resources in any moment depends on their pressing interests and motivations and some classroom social drama. So the goal is to get in the flow of the children; in Hamel's words, we have to "attach to energy and motivation already present . . . rather than replacing it with an adult goal or standard." Composing, after all, is an intentional act; no control over intentions, no engagement with its semiotic potential.

So how do we as teachers come to know children's agendas? What tensions might we experience if their motivations or resources are other than what we had in mind? These are the fundamental questions that energize this book. And the stories of intentional children in their situated moments illuminate the stories they write. Hamel comes to know these human stories—these children as bundles of motivations, interests, insecurities, and assurances—by listening. This deceptively simple pedagogical move also echoes Ashton-Warner: "From the teacher's end it boils down to whether or not [one] is a good conversationalist, whether or not [one] has the gift or the wisdom to listen to another" (Ashton-Warner, 1963, p. 58).

This is not so easy to do, this listening. As a reflective volunteer, a writing teacher/observer in Mr. Allegro's class, Hamel allows us into his teacher reflections and tensions. Imagine, for example, a teacher, Mr. Hamel in particular, resisting the urge to tell a young writer named Macie that her story about a mother cat and her baby kitty must hang in a coherent way; I imagine this urge is physical, the adult hand wanting badly to make arrows, swirls, and carets on Macie's paper. We teachers have been there. If he instead feeds into Macie's intense participation by asking questions about *her* sense of her story, where it has been and where she might go, is he failing to teach Macie, or is he helping her down her writing road? After all, we don't want to yank away Macie's motivations and interests; she was painting a large life canvas where babies grew up, lost and became mothers, and bravely faced unexpected challenges, even at just 16 years old. Moreover, if we interrupt rather than engage with her flow, Macie might lose the agency and spunk she showed in sticking to her story and searching for sources of new happenings and responses from her peers.

And so we negotiate through our teaching days. It must be said that Ashton-Warner had a confidence that I have never had as a teacher. I listen and react because I have to. Later, I think it all over and anticipate what I hope will happen next. Fred Hamel not only offers us readers insight into the text-mediated dramas of children's lives, he allows us into the sort of pedagogical reflections that keep us all in the flow of becoming.

So put on your swimming goggles and dive in.

—*Anne Haas Dyson*

REFERENCE

Ashton-Warner, S. (1963). *Teacher*. London, England: Secker and Warburg.

Acknowledgments

I'm fortunate to be part of a vibrant and experienced learning community at the University of Puget Sound—one that sustains my growth and, in many ways, has made this project possible. I'm especially grateful to my faculty colleagues in the School of Education—Amy Ryken, Terry Beck, John Woodward, Molly Pugh, and Mary Boer—all inspiring educators—for challenging and nurturing me. For several years, Amy Ryken sent her undergraduate students to observe in the writers' workshop described in this book. Terry Beck offered guidance with my early conceptualizations and has been an ongoing source of support. Thanks go to Mary Boer, colleague and remarkable 5th-grade teacher, for reading several chapters and offering keen, insightful feedback. I thank other colleagues I have worked with closely through the School of Education—Barbara Holme, Jennice King, Heather Jaasko, Susie Askew, Christine Kline, Carol Frankl, Karen Stump, and Anna Coy. Each has supported me in substantial ways as a teacher educator. Beyond these individuals, I am thankful for the institutional support I received from the university, which allowed me to step away from teaching and other duties to write in a sustained way.

I'm grateful to Emily Spangler at Teachers College Press for her willingness to advocate for this project and for her skilled support. Since our initial conversation in Vancouver, British Columbia, in 2012, Emily understood my timeline and provided just the right amount of guidance—precise, steady, encouraging, and informed. I thank the reviewers who positively evaluated my proposal, those readers who provided critical feedback on the manuscript, and all others at TCP who have so competently contributed to the final production.

I acknowledge and honor my original graduate school mentors in the field of education, Pamela Grossman, dean of the Graduate School of Education at the University of Pennsylvania, and George Hillocks Jr., professor emeritus of the University of Chicago, who passed away in 2014. These remarkable leaders and researchers brought me into the field of teaching and teacher education—and cultivated in me a love for literacy and the teaching of writing. George, of course, was a critic of writing workshops in many ways, but my hope is that George would recognize within these pages much of the generous spirit, and love of learners and learning, that I acquired from him.

A large share of thanks goes to the teachers and administrators at Adams Elementary School (a pseudonym), where the events of this book take place. The school staff was tremendously welcoming, supportive, and genuinely interested in what was occurring in the 4th grade where I spent most of my time. I gained as much from several parents at Adams who, over 5 years, showed up to volunteer in the classroom. Our many conversations about children and writing were refreshing and perspective-changing. Of course, I also thank the students at Adams whom I was blessed to work with and to know. Your creative spirit and willingness to experiment and play with writing are the driving forces behind this book.

My central experience throughout this project has been with Samuel Allegro, 4th-grade teacher at Adams. I cannot offer enough gratitude and respect to Sam for simply being open to this work, for his skilled teaching and deep care of children, for his magnanimous spirit and big laugh, and for graciously letting me enter into the flow of his classroom space. Our collaboration and many conversations have, over the years, become a living friendship. Coming into your classroom, Sam, each week for so many years, altered my understanding of children and writing. I owe you a great deal.

This project originally started when my own children, Teddi and Will, were in 7th and 4th grades, respectively. They are now young adults. Observing their growth and change over the past 10-plus years, their "becoming" new independent persons, fills me with immense pride and continues to transform my life. Teddi hosted me in Winthrop, WA, during a snowy January 2016, as I started off sabbatical and launched the sustained writing of this book. Will participated in workshop as a 4th-grader during our very first year and, as I completed the manuscript in August 2016, offered generous, perceptive feedback. Teddi and Will, I hope you each know how much you inspire me, bless my life, and make me happy as you pursue your own pathways.

There is one person to whom I dedicate this book—and for whom I truly cannot find adequate words to thank. My life partner and spouse, Trinka Ross Hamel, has been my sage and companion throughout. Trinka, you are woven into the soul of this work. During the earliest phases of workshop, you advised Mr. Allegro and me on ways to think about the range of young writers we were observing. As a learning specialist in schools, you offered insights into the kinds of environments in which these students might best thrive. You volunteered regularly during the first year and modeled generous support to writers. Years later, when I decided to contact Teachers College Press, unsure how to write such a book, you provided unfailing encouragement and support. You read each chapter as it emerged, providing sensitive, attuned feedback and critique—helping me through my writing shoals and pushing my thoughts further. You read the chapters again. This book, in short, would not be what it is without you—or more honestly, it would not *be* without you. It has been a joy to take so many life steps together, and I am thankful to be on a remarkable life journey with you.

Introduction

THE ORIGINS OF A WRITERS' WORKSHOP WITH UPPER ELEMENTARY STUDENTS

In the fall of 2002, my wife and I met with our son's 4th-grade teacher to discuss his learning. That summer, we had moved from a different community, 35 miles away, as I changed jobs, and our children had experienced the challenge of losing their familiar neighborhood and starting again in new schools. As part of the conversation with his new teacher, we emphasized that our son, Will, had enjoyed writing when he was a 3rd-grader. With one of his best friends, he had spent untold hours composing lengthy, whimsical narratives about two birds—curiously named "Foo" and "Fu"—based on two parakeets we owned as pets. Given wide latitude to compose and create together in his 3rd-grade classroom, Will and his friend daily invented scenes, experimented with language and voice, played with perspective, and made humorous observations about the world. Near the end of the year, my wife typed up the work—eventually titled *Fluff*—and made copies. *Fluff* became, for a time, essential nighttime reading at our home.

As we shared this experience, our son's new teacher, Mr. Sam Allegro,[1] generously signaled interest. He showed great care for our son, interest in writing as a mode of learning, and, as we talked, a desire to revisit the linear, step-by-step approaches to writing often encountered in upper elementary grades. Together, we acknowledged a desire to move, if possible, beyond some of the more prescribed forms of literacy instruction that were becoming common, especially in larger, urban school districts, at the time. In reading, for example, scripted, teacher-directed instruction, focused on form, accuracy, and fluency, was becoming a norm. Together, we hoped for something different and less rigidly controlled. We even envisioned a scenario where students would locate their own writing topics, purposes, needs, and audiences, with emphasis on student-driven communication, meaning-making, and writer identity—and where adults would make space for writers to experiment with language. This seemed well out of tune with recent curricular developments, but it was good to imagine at the time.

Such were the origins of the writers' workshop around which this book revolves. For 5 years, I served as a volunteer as Mr. Allegro "tried on" a writing workshop in his classroom, usually for just a couple of hours a week, within an otherwise regulated literacy context (that is, with the curriculum prescribed and actively monitored). During our second year, one of Mr. Allegro's 5th-grade colleagues decided to try conducting a writing workshop as well—partly because of requests from students who had been in Mr. Allegro's class the year before. Partly, too, from parents who began to ask about "that writing thing" happening in his classroom. Each year, Mr. Allegro invited parent volunteers to participate and occasionally opened the class up to observing students from the local university where I taught literacy-related education courses. Along the way, I realized my own intrigue with what was happening, received university approval to conduct research in Mr. Allegro's classroom, and nearly every week I would sit down to write up what I had experienced as a participant-observer.

I share these reflections to highlight that this book has personal roots, and that my involvement has always been more than just a matter of academic research. My stance reflects investment and personal connection to the teacher, school, community, and students with whom I engaged, and the voice I take on is not analytically distant. I rely upon narrative to capture the affect and character of moment-to-moment experiences, and my interweaving perspectives as parent, professor, teacher, and school volunteer have energized the project for me.

What follows is thus not a prescription for how to teach writing or how to conduct a workshop. It emphasizes instead close description of student practice in a flexible, dynamic context. Mike Rose (2014) reminds us of the importance of

> staying close to the ground, of finding out what people are thinking, of trying our best—flawed though it will be—to understand the world as they see it . . . and to be ready to revise our understanding. This often means taking another line of sight on what seems familiar, seeing things in a new light. (p. 3)

As Rose suggests, we may never fully understand students' motives, and our interpretations will always be incomplete in some way. Yet, trying on "another line of sight" and seeking to ascertain purposes and motives from the learner's perspective—these are powerful practices, ones that students greatly need from the adults around them. For educators, what results is an enhanced ability to engage, interpret, and support young learners over time.

Overall, this work strives for a connected and empathetic stance toward young writers, one facilitated by my own role in Mr. Allegro's classroom, even as I bring educational theory and writing research to bear on my observations. I endorse Rose's (2014) view that the work of seeing students up close may be a "precondition for creating an effective and truly democratic school reform" (p. 68). Using a unique vantage point as volunteer, academic, and invested parent, I raise questions about what energizes students within literate worlds and what we imagine writing to be, both intellectually and affectively, as we frame efforts to support literacy development within and beyond the classroom.

THE GOALS OF THIS BOOK

The pages that follow present narrative portraits of upper elementary students developing and negotiating their abilities, identities, and social worlds as writers in a workshop context that offered significant choice and authority to participants. Drawing on my own role as participant-observer over the course of 5 years, including data from some 60 descriptive journal entries, I aim to help educators consider the importance of experimentation, flexibility, and identity in shaping writing experiences for upper elementary learners. I assert an argument—namely, that young writers need access to flexible and self-directed writing environments, with opportunities for choice, social interaction, and physical movement, in order to locate and make visible learning zones that are constructive for their growth. (I use the term *learning zone* in a Vygotskian [1978] sense, to refer to a space of growth that reflects learners' potential achievement with the assistance of others in a social context.) Too often, students' potential development is assumed, defined, and/ or dominated by adult perceptions, or by curricular materials, such that students themselves struggle to be seen and heard as learners. Flexibly structured environments, I suggest, though not a panacea, help students show themselves to us in new ways and allow us to extend our ways of learning *from* students. Such contexts, further, assist us in questioning what we *mean* by writing and literacy growth for young learners.

This book also offers potentially new representations of students as learners, extending our usual assumptions about what writing is and how upper elementary writers might learn. Environments that offer flexible room for writing exploration, I assert, can help learners find their own footing and experiment with new roles, identities, and strategies in the context of meaningful communication. Such contexts require new forms of expertise from adults. Particularly in a standards-driven era, students need classroom teachers who are able to see, appreciate, build on, and advocate for learners' emergent strengths and starting points—that is, who productively meet learners where they are. Developing such observational capacities and values is especially important as we respond to writers whose writing attempts surprise us, are harder to understand, or seem to fall outside our usual expectations.

In what follows, I make visible what drew students' energies in a choice-oriented environment, what practices and outcomes emerged, what tensions we experienced, and what forms of growth occurred, with the aim of helping teachers realistically envision new practices and more richly make sense of students' writing initiatives. Specifically, I hope to:

- provide concrete, palpable images of a less traditional context for writing, in which upper elementary students were encouraged to choose topics, genres, timelines, and resources based on their own needs and interests;
- clarify the principles and practices that grounded our workshop setting, which stood in contrast to the usual district literacy curriculum students experienced;
- illustrate ways in which flexible parameters and choice revealed less common dimensions of students' writing development;
- document the dilemmas, fears, and challenges that adults and students faced in the writing environment we created; and
- advocate for greater respect for the developmental worlds of young writers, raising questions about standards, curricula, and pedagogy that may too narrowly and too often control the writing experiences of elementary learners.

Readers of this book, I hope, will become more skilled observers of children's literacy learning, increasingly sensitive to the nuances of student motivation and desire, classroom environment and relationships, and adult expectation and input. Few observational studies devote themselves to such goals with upper elementary learners, compared, for example, with early childhood or primary-age students, where the lion's share of research on writing seems to occur. Upper elementary students, who are often still making sense of their new literacy abilities in a media-intensive world, are under significant pressure today to be readied for rigorous, academic, adult-oriented standards—to be socialized into academic essay writing (Gee, 2001) and relatively narrow forms of creative writing, typically restricted to individualistic first-person narrative (Hillocks, 2002). Even Calkins's recent and extensive workshop-based curriculum (Calkins, 2010; Calkins, Ehrenworth, & Lehman, 2012), responding to the Common Core State Standards, emphasizes leading upper elementary students through particular writing modes in "roughly synchronized" ways. Elementary students live today under increasing expectations, even in otherwise humane classroom settings, to proceed and learn on adult-constructed timelines.

This work, conversely, demonstrates how 4th-graders' writing practices emerged in an environment with greater space for self-determination, less tied to endpoints, and open to unexpected writer initiatives. It explores both possibility and tension in offering such flexibility, choice, and scope with upper elementary learners. As I try to show in the chapters that follow, students can benefit from opportunities to identify their own writing needs and desires—potentially increasing their motivation, sense of purpose, and sense of writer identity within a community of learners. I argue, ultimately, that such an approach to writing—one that remains open to students' self-driven initiatives—takes listening, courage, and a willingness among adults to apprentice themselves to children's dynamic ways with language.

AUDIENCE AND CHAPTER OVERVIEW

In what follows, I describe various forms of student activity in Mr. Allegro's writing workshop, through my own lens as a classroom volunteer. I write with varied readers in mind, including elementary school teachers interested in trying on new stances and approaches with writing and/or seeking to reflect on the writing practices of their students. Such teachers, I hope, will be able to identify with the child-centered portraits, as well as with the tentative, exploratory teacher thinking that I share. A second intended audience involves preservice teachers and other education students hoping to learn about children's literacy development. Along with these I include parents as well, especially those wondering about a child's writing growth and how it may fit within school expectations. Finally, I write for teacher educators, those hoping to assist adult learners in imagining writing interactions in new ways and in reflecting upon and filtering the messages of methods textbooks, curriculum materials, and classroom observations. For all, I encourage reflection on the interests, strengths, and purposes of emerging upper elementary writers, especially in relationship to existing writing curricula.

Chapter 1, "Initiating a New Writing Environment: Perspective and Practice," offers a theoretical and practical foundation for the workshop described in this book. The chapter grounds readers in a brief opening narrative, describing how Mr. Allegro and I worked with students to get workshop started on one of our first days. It discusses the theories that guided the formation of our workshop and that shape my observations throughout the book. The chapter then lays out the design of our writing environment and the practical approach we used in supporting writers. Finally, it reflects on the context of our work, which took place in a middle-class school in an urban district.

Chapters 2 through 6, the heart of the book, offer detailed narrative accounts of my interactions with students around a range of unconventional themes—unconventional in the sense that they focus less on best practices or concrete writing outcomes and more on intriguing and unexpected student practices that emerged. In this sense, these chapters convey what was most surprising and remarkable to me as an adult in Mr. Allegro's room. Each of these chapters concludes with questions for reflection to support ongoing reader consideration.

Chapter 2, "Writing as Visualizing Popular Worlds," focuses on three students, Martin, Carla, and Ricky, who used visual imagination and drawing extensively, and differently, in order to participate in the workshop. The chapter describes my own efforts to provide support, to ascertain these students' goals and needs, and to understand the fusion of popular culture in their drawing/writing attempts. I emphasize how, rather than a distraction, visual engagement with popular worlds became, for these students, a means of thinking and a way to enter into writing processes and community meaningfully.

Chapter 3, "Conferencing and Literacy Desiring: Trusting Students as Writers," highlights my attempts to engage with writers in conferences, especially where I found myself struggling to support students whose writing goals differed from my own. The chapter describes my efforts to encourage two girls to revise a Valentine's Day story they had written together, and it recounts my struggles and concerns with another student whose writing seemed simply confusing. In both cases, I strive to listen, understand, and latch on to students' "literacy desiring," even as this challenged my usual aims and assumptions about writing.

Chapter 4, "How Relationships Influence Writing and Writing Influences Relationships," argues that writing in our workshop was entangled with relational needs and goals. Writing was not simply about genres, ideas, skills, and products. Instead, students used their writing to manage relationships and make social gestures. Writing events were occasions to reach across boundaries to classmates and to navigate voice, control, and status as students worked together. Relationships nurtured, motivated, and sometimes complicated writing—and writing practices, conversely, were tools to achieve a range of interpersonal goals.

Chapter 5, "Sharing and Publishing: Being Seen, Heard, and Valued," describes how workshop routines for making writing "visible" in the classroom (for example, students sharing their writing aloud with the entire class or creating "publications" for the class library) motivated ongoing writing initiatives among students, even as students navigated the risks of public exposure. I illustrate how sharing and publishing routines, depending upon the stances taken by adults, had the power to confer validation and inclusion in the classroom—that is, full writing membership, particularly with students otherwise easily labeled "below standard" in writing.

Chapter 6, "Shaping the Writing Curriculum Together," offers two accounts of whole-class interaction. In the first, which takes place during a minilesson, students use their own writing initiatives to challenge what the notion of "plot" might mean. In the second, Mr. Allegro opens up a class conversation on a day when writing with disturbing content is shared publicly before the group. I argue that our workshop offered an environment where students gained important forms of agency, not just with individual pieces of writing but in relation to the writing curriculum itself. Such shared conversations required a responsive and dialogic stance on the part of adults, which was not without tension and challenge.

The final chapter, Chapter 7, "Developing Children as Writers," offers conceptual and practical implications, emphasizing the importance of allowing elementary students to become literate "as kids." I encourage educators to reconsider how we define teacher expertise and emphasize the importance of moving beyond a linear application of standards. I urge teachers to leverage their own unparalleled presence with children and to respect what students are "chasing after" in their writing efforts. I underscore the ethical implications of listening carefully to student practices, offering specific questions that teachers might apply in their own classroom spaces.

CHAPTER 1

Initiating a New Writing Environment

Perspective and Practice

DAY ONE

January 6: It's day one of writers' workshop with a new class of 4th-grade students. Over the past 2 years, Mr. Allegro and I have developed a first-day sequence to orient students to the environment we will establish. There is energy in the air, with a couple of guests in the room—a parent volunteer and myself. Mr. Allegro and I lead the first day together. He is the central figure, but he generously makes space for me to interact with students and get to know them. We begin by asking: "What comes to mind when you hear the term workshop? What associations do you have with this word?"

Students take up the question and mention ideas like "building things together." One says, "It's like the place where my dad works." Mr. Allegro has kids say their names aloud when answering, which helps me as a new-comer. One boy likens workshop to an art studio—with open space and lots of resources.

Another mentions "Santa's workshop," and Mr. Allegro goes with this, asking what students imagine that to be like. A few hesitate, as if they know too much, but others call out that it's "busy" and that there are "lots of tools."

Mr. Allegro asks rhetorically: "Does everyone work on the same thing at the same time?"

Several students respond with the expected "no," and a few others look thoughtful, as if realizing how often schooling does, in fact, involve doing the same things at once. Mr. Allegro says that a workshop is a busy place, with people doing different things, and it's sometimes a little noisy.

One of our main goals on this first day is to help shift students' conception of classroom space and activity—to reconsider their own agency and roles in the room. We use the term *workshop* itself for this, and students' personal associations with the word are valuable. Some theorists question the very word *workshop*, however, finding it limiting, and instead favoring language with alternative connotations—such as *playshops* (Wohlwend,

2011, 2013) or *studio* (Kuby & Gutshall Rucker, 2015). Harper (2010) notes that the word *workshop* has "long carried with it the holistic sense of object production, as well as its more specific association with small manufacturing" (p. xvii). *Workshop*, Harper writes, "has long been associated with something to be done in order to produce something to be valued" (p. xvii). Such comments positively describe our aims—we want students to produce something valuable—but also raise good questions about what is intended in workshop settings. Indeed, our own workshop, as explained below, gained force not merely through final products but at least as much through moment-to-moment experiences, experimentation, and relationships.

Mr. Allegro next asks the class: "What happens in a *writing* workshop? What kinds of things will we do?" Several kids again respond, focusing mainly on topics they might write about, such as having the freedom to write about dinosaurs and other personal interests. Several topics emerge, and we emphasize that our workshop will allow choice regarding topics and also in the *kinds* of writing students will do. We say that in school teachers very often *give* writing assignments and indicate what, or how, to write—but this workshop will be a little unusual, more open. We clarify that students can work with partners of their choosing, as long as everyone agrees, and that they will be able to move around the classroom, with the caveat that we will intervene if a problem is not being resolved. Mr. Allegro notes that, in past years, some students have found partnering exceptionally beneficial, while others have found it enticing at first but then more challenging. We say that if they want to create groups with more than two people, they need to check in first with Mr. Allegro.

Finally, we indicate that students can determine their own timeline for writing, noting that students in previous years have worked on projects for just a week, while others have developed pieces over the course of months. In other words, Mr. Allegro will be less concerned about getting students to a particular writing "place" within a particular time frame. Our workshop will allow students to have significant input on where their work begins and ends. As we talk, students take this point in stride. Nothing about it appears to strike them as particularly extreme, although it is well out of tune with most school-based writing instruction.

Next, a few students from last year's class show up, as arranged with their 5th-grade teacher. Danni, Bridget, Ronny, Marisa, and Shayna share their memories from the workshop last year. They talk about their own projects and who they worked with. Danni talks about how she needed to take a break from her story, and her partner, when writing together got too hard. Ronny recalls "SuperFlea," his opus work, and how he got lots of help keyboarding, eventually deciding only to do Part One, and to drop Part Two, because Part One was a lot more work than he realized. Marisa notes how she enjoyed working in the hallway and with different partners over time. Shayna mentions being able to write about anything—as she did in her story, "A Day in the Life of Cheese." Danni shares how sometimes students wrote during recess, because they were still "into thought," as she puts it, when the bell rang. We thank these students as they leave, and Mr. Allegro and I display a few artifacts from previous years—classroom publications, drafts, and artwork—leaving these out for students to look through later.

Our little orientation is almost over. There are more basics to share in the coming days, but this is enough for now. I ask: "Does anyone *already* have an idea of what they might want to write about?" I indicate that it usually takes me a while to figure out my own writing ideas, but I'm curious to find out if anything is emerging. Over half the students raise their hands. This is a pattern from previous years: Given a bit of freedom, many 4th-graders in Mr. Allegro's class do not seem to have difficulty generating sparks for ideas; many are brimming with possible directions, pet interests, even projects already in motion. In other words, the juices are already flowing, in and around the given curriculum, seemingly well before the idea of workshop even arrived. Such students, indeed, experience relief and energy when they are allowed to pursue their own ideas in the classroom. But this is not true of all students. A few can be thrown off, as if having flexible space, time, and choice conflicts too much with what they've learned about being in school. Such students will legitimately struggle to find ideas or won't know where to start. But a high percentage, a critical mass of students each year, experiences palpable relief.

Students are eager to begin, and we give them two concrete parameters: They can move around in the classroom, but the hallway is off-limits, at least for this first week. We also clarify about noise. Showing students a vertical scale of 1 (complete silence) to 5 (recess voice), we ask them what a good noise level would probably be for workshop. A few venture to say 3, and we say that today we will shoot for 2.5. Everyone seems okay with this, and we indicate that we will give reminders if needed. Mr. Allegro and I have become better, more confident, in the past 2 years, in asserting a few basic management pieces that help the workshop function. With that, Mr. Allegro says, "Okay, it's workshop time," and we start.

* * *

Throughout this book, I emphasize that writing environments that support experimentation, flexibility, and identity are important in helping adults understand "where kids are" in their development and who they are becoming as language users. In this chapter, building from the scene above, I briefly explain the theoretical ideas that informed our workshop design; describe the concrete structures and practices we used in the classroom; and comment on the context of the school in which I worked. I do not claim that our workshop was or is the only kind of writing environment that students should experience. There is likely no single solution to the complex question of "how" to teach writing—though some of my leanings toward specific methods and practices come through in the chapters that follow. Elementary teachers work in complex environments with increasingly intensified demands, which sometimes shape hybrid teaching practices with competing theoretical orientations. I do not argue that our environment was without difficulty, tension, or challenges. My point, rather, is that young writers need instructional responsiveness, a kind of curricular "flex" (Genishi, 2016) that goes beyond ready-made goals, genres, and processes. Such responsiveness makes room for what upper elementary writers *bring* to language events. Without such a stance, in an era of heightened standards, and especially for those students marginalized by the literacy practices of schools, we risk losing track of the nuanced ways in which young people learn and develop as writers.

THEORETICAL FOUNDATIONS

Background

Mr. Allegro and I did not explicitly discuss the theories behind our workshop before we started; instead, we talked about new arrangements in the classroom and concrete practices, many of which I share later in this chapter. The theoretical foundations were more like incipient beliefs, hovering beneath the surface. Making such concepts explicit has been, in some ways, an outgrowth of practice, generated along the way or after the fact. To state it up front, however, our underlying foundation was social constructivist, though rarely had I seen a classroom grounded genuinely in social constructivism, despite the very many classrooms I had visited in my university role as a teacher educator.

Mr. Allegro, for his part, had been teaching for 21 years when we began working together, though he was only in his second year at Adams Elementary. He had a personal affinity for writing and was in the process of creating a children's book himself. It was disappointing to him that writing had become an afterthought in the district curriculum under the weight of reading reform guided by No Child Left Behind. He was intrigued by new ways of approaching writing instruction and expressed a desire to do "more" with writing in the classroom, beyond the direct instruction that is commonly assumed and practiced at his grade level (Anderson & Dryden, 2014). As he told me:

> I always felt like, in order to do a good job of teaching writing, you needed that, that intimacy level of being connected in conference style

with kids, rather than saying, okay, today we're going to write about whatever, and then, okay, now we're done, pass your papers in, and I'll put some comments down on a piece of paper. So much gets lost there.

Mr. Allegro was concerned about writing experiences where students experience low investment or a lack of connection to what they are writing. He believed that students need informal engagements, active conferencing, and "intimacy" with writing, as he put it.

Yet decentralizing control in the classroom and giving students greater space and freedom was not easy. He had learned briefly about workshop models in his own past teacher education, but had never carried things very far. He recalled that in one early career attempt with workshop, he possessed a tendency to get so involved in conferencing with individual students that he lost track of others. The memory had stayed with him. Workshops could be unpredictable, hard to manage. He also shared with me another perception or fear—namely that the vigilant middle-class parents at his new school (he had worked in schools with greater racial and socioeconomic diversity than Adams for most of his career) might find workshop too "loosy-goosy"—not rigorous enough. Mr. Allegro did not feel particularly secure in "opening up" the writing curriculum, at least on his own, even though he believed doing so might serve students well.

Learning as Participation: Growth in Flexibly Organized Environments

In spite of these fears, and with the support of my spouse, who had experience with workshop settings as an inclusion support specialist, we tried something new—something social constructivist in nature. Social constructivism emphasizes the ways in which ideas, practices, experiences, and products are constructed within communities, stressing the role of cultural context, social dynamics, and mediational tools such as interactive dialogue and material artifacts. Different from "cognitive constructivism," which characterized my own teacher preparation background (Bereiter & Scardamalia, 1987), social constructivism conceives of learning less as "thinking" and more in terms of social mediation (Lave & Wenger, 1991; Rogoff, 2003; Vygotsky, 1978. For a useful source distinguishing a range of literacy theories, including cognitive and social constructivism, with practical illustrations, see Handsfield, 2016.) Rogoff (1994), for example, frames learning within a social-constructivist paradigm as "transformation of participation." Here, Rogoff removes the concept of learning from being either "teacher-centered" or "child-centered," shifting the idea of development from an internal intellectual process of thinking, or acquisition of skills, to one of ongoing membership and activity ("participation") within a community. Learning is fundamentally about being a *part* of something—being transformed through shared activity. This contrasts with our usual sense of learning as "attaining" something, intellectually and individually, such as discrete knowledge or skills.

Social constructivists highlight how the imperatives of social member-ship and interaction drive change—that participation in communities can "transform" over time. Rogoff (1998), for example, argues that, when we are immersed in ongoing, socially driven processes, we are propelled by the imperatives of the environment; we change in response to "the situ-ation at hand" (p. 690), in relation to the immediacy of physical materi-als, the purposefulness of our involvement, and through social interactions that emerge between participants. Learning, from a social-constructivist perspective, does not have to be linear, adult-directed, or technically or-dered. As learners, we often grow in flexibly organized environments, such as family settings or informal cultural contexts, where shared purposes and endeavors drive growth. We are "stretched" by the "communication and coordination" (p. 690) required as different roles come into contact and as new perspectives and actions are experienced and negotiated.

Many of the fundamental decisions Mr. Allegro and I made around our workshop reflected a social-constructivist perspective, even if we were not especially conscious of it at the time. We set up materials, space, and conditions to emphasize a collaborative writing experience, through which all members could join in the practices of writing. We framed learning pri-marily as meaningful participation in the environment, more so than around our own teaching designs or around assessing how well products matched up with pre-established standards. Our shared goals were for students to experiment with their developing capacities with language and print, to use their own interests and experiences as the stuff of communication, and to see one another as interested audiences. This does not mean that we never provided direction, used our expertise, modeled, or established parameters, but our notions of student success and learning revolved around *changing forms of participation*—cases of which I describe in the chapters that follow.

This is not to argue that learning *only* occurs in explicitly designed, com-munity-of-learners settings. Learning occurs in various ways, contexts, and arrangements, including in more traditional, teacher-directed instruction. Social constructivists make the point, however, that the nature of "what is learned" in directed or teacher-centered approaches may differ from what is formally intended, as sociocultural forces and student agency shape the learning arena (on this point, with respect to children's writing, see especial-ly Dyson, 1997, 2003, 2013). Moreover, alternative instructional models shape "different relations of the learner to the information and its uses . . . and to the community in which the information is regarded as important" (Rogoff, 1994, pp. 210–211). In other words, learning models shape how individuals "relate to" what they are learning—how they regard it and what place it might take in their lives. Put simply, learner identities and motivations are involved.

Writing as Play and Exploration: Attending to the Moment

A second framing of our workshop is captured in relatively recent literacy research, which challenges the ways in which even progressive theory remains guided by assumptions of "rational design" and "well-intentioned hope for control" (Leander & Boldt, 2012, pp. 24, 33). In this critical perspective, the primary goal of writing instruction is too often to engineer specific, expected products from children, rather than to make space for the emergence of something new, creative, or unexpected. Writing curriculum and research are dominated by a sense of expected textual outcome and a narrow "text-centric perspective" (p. 33), which often hides from view the ways in which literacy is lived and experienced by children. Leander and Boldt (2012) describe the problem:

> our vision is fixed on a future goal; teachers' and students' investments and practices are measured in relation to some intentional design or intervention that leads to an imagined point in the future. The dynamic unfolding of living practices is dominated by a future conception of their desired results or effects, rather than through their affectivities in the dynamics of living practice. (p. 34)

These researchers signal the importance of attending to "the dynamics of living practice," to the ways in which learners interact with and draw meanings from, and with, texts and textual situations—in the moment. They argue that our understanding of writers and writing itself is diminished by a restricted focus on "desired results." A preoccupation with future goals, and even purely textual goals, too often eclipses what kids are doing and accomplishing through literacy, often removing us, crucially, from their emotional resonances and experiences, their "affectivities."

Within this framework, Boldt (2009) retrieves Britton's (1970) nearly 50-year-old critique that writing instruction and research focus too heavily on "the child's production of writing for a critical audience" rather than on children's uses of writing for "exploring and experimenting with the nature of reality . . . for the development of creativity and an appreciation of social diversity" (Boldt, p. 11). Recovering the notion of "play," Boldt (2009) writes that children use writing for purposes that are sometimes obscure to adults, yet often allow young people to grapple with their lived experience: "to reflect or work upon inner and outer experiences and meanings" (p. 13). Boldt (2009) comments on the writing of 6-year-old Kyle, whose brief lines in invented spelling about an evil serpent (a "basilisk") are drawn from watching a Harry Potter movie:

Kyle does not intend his writing to function as a well-crafted text. Rather, we might understand Kyle as creating his text in an attempt to consider and negotiate the experiences and meanings he found in a movie that both captivated and frightened him. . . . He has no interest in using this as an opportunity to learn to spell more conventionally nor does he want to revise his writing with more attention to audience concerns. (pp. 13, 15)

Boldt (2009) asks teachers to remain open to, and provide opportunity for, Kyle's own meanings and purposes in writing, especially by providing writers with "the necessary gift of time and space" (p. 17). A teacher with this stance, Boldt writes, "offers [students] an environment replete with opportunities to play and work with her/his own fantasies and theories while immersed in the talk and concerns of others" (p. 14). This allows the child to "come to know and integrate more of the realities and demands of the external world" (p. 15). Children, in other words, need time to integrate and filter the many inputs and experiences of their lives, which is a fundamental purpose of writing, at least as much as the formation of final products.

One assertion I make here is that the need for such time, space, play, and experimentation (see also Wohlwend, 2015) does not disappear as children get a bit older. Indeed, we often associate such an emphasis on play and exploration exclusively with very young writers, with early childhood literacy education and primary school classrooms. One thing that made our workshop distinct is precisely that it applied such assumptions to older elementary learners—giving greater commitment to opportunities for self-determination with 8- to 11-year-olds, putting less emphasis on expected endpoints. Running against the grain, even for just a few hours a week, our workshop functioned as a kind of experimental site for challenging a common assumption: that flexible, choice-oriented writing, less focused on teacher-directed guidance and structured outcomes, is not fitting for such "older" elementary students. We asked instead: What did our learners *do* with the space, time, and flexibility we offered? And what could we learn from them in the process?

OUR WRITERS' WORKSHOP APPROACH

Observations from the First Day

Let's return to the classroom for a moment, right after Mr. Allegro and I had launched our workshop on the first day described above. My purpose in returning to this scene, besides keeping us connected to students in the classroom, is to give a sense of the fluid movement characteristic of our workshop space, as well as to comment on my own writing and observational role in the classroom.

January 6, continued: The writers' workshop begins, and I notice kids getting up, moving to sharpen pencils, looking at magazines, gathering around Mr. Allegro with questions, sitting and thinking, and meeting with partners in the idea center. Erik sits by himself at first, seemingly without an idea but contemplating. Maria starts reading through a few published stories from last year, which we've laid around. After a while she has written down the word sapphire, spelled "saphire," on paper and then after a few moments holds it out in front of her, saying aloud: "Does anybody want to use the word saphire?"

One boy comes up to me to say he's writing a story at home, and he's in the middle of chapter 2. He says he'll try starting chapter 3 here at school and will fill in the rest of chapter 2 later. After this revelation, he goes back to his desk, intent on his work.

Erik pairs up with Shaun, and they decide they want to do something with superheroes. I overhear them say that maybe Erik will "be" the super-hero.

Jerry, sitting near the front whiteboard, shows me a cartoon dog he's traced, which he refers to as "Superdog." He seems to have picked up on 5th-grader Ronny's "SuperFlea" motif from the guest presentation. I sit with Jerry, watching him draw a dog tag under Superdog's neck, writing "SD" on it. I encourage him, building on the visual. "Does the dog tag have super-powers?"

> *Jerry:* Oh yeah, it could be a laser that makes something small.
> *Me:* Or it stuns them.
> *Jerry:* Yeah.
> *Me:* What if he had a bone? What would that be?

We keep working with our dog associations and soon are talking about whether Superdog has a leash. Jerry decides that the leash could be Super-dog's "evil nemesis." As he looks at his drawing, he studies the dog collar that holds the dog tag, saying, "Maybe it's a boomerang."

Maria keeps reading student stories from last year's workshop. At one point, she calls out, holding up a classroom publication: "Anybody want to read 'The Mystery of the Golden Spatula'?" Another boy is writing about an iguana independently. His story has many misspellings. The first sentence includes the color of the iguana: *saphire.* The iguana goes out and meets other creatures and makes friends with a frog; they exchange names, "pencil" and "gold." Then the iguana goes home. This all occurs in less than one page, written out in pencil. At the bottom, the boy skips a space and has written: "Chapter 2." He tells me: "I don't know what that part will be yet."

My Role and Viewpoint in the Classroom

This brief snapshot makes visible a few points about my own lens for observing in the classroom and in the chapters that follow. First, I recorded my observations in the midst of helping kids with their work. I typically walked around with a small writing notebook, and between interactions or when students did not have immediate needs, I would jot down concrete observations, recording key words, descriptions, as well as my own thoughts. After workshop, I would use my jotted notes and immediate memory to flesh out the details as soon as possible, usually the same day. Doing so allowed me to create running accounts of what I had observed and experienced. My notes often capture, as above, a succession of brief interactions, observations, or bits and pieces as I moved around the room. Other times, they involve more sustained engagements with particular students. The chapters that follow thus reflect my own experiences and observations with children, more so than those of Mr. Allegro, his thinking, or his experience per se, although he was a constant presence for everything I did in the room, and we consulted and interacted regularly.

Another aspect of my lens relates to tone. My voice and disposition in writing reflects my role as a parent volunteer, as someone invested in the school and known to some of the students and their parents. This hybrid role (parent, professor, volunteer) changed the nature of my experience as a researcher, creating a more personal, less clinical stance—one I might characterize as generous and even hopeful toward the work of students. Dahlberg and Moss (2009) refer to reestablishing "an affirming and experimenting attitude" (p. xiv) with regard to children's lives in schools, which captures the stance to which I aspired. From this vantage point, I was most interested in seeing students in light of their own purposes and encounters with writing. How did students' writing actions and behavior make sense to them? How did they use the workshop to *do* things, relationally, with and through writing? How should we understand Maria's efforts to distribute an intriguing word, *saphire (sapphire)*, to her classmates? What draws Jerry to the cartoonish superhero genre, "Superdog," so readily? My observations, in this respect, focus on "the new, the interesting, and the remarkable," as opposed to "the controlling of parameters" or "the expected outcome" (Olsson, 2009, p. 28). My narrative attempts, in many ways, reflect a personal effort to work on this kind of imagination with children, struggling with it at times and trying to become better at it.

A generous stance does not mean that I refrain from challenges, fears, and dilemmas. Mr. Allegro and I were not always sure what direction to take or how to respond to situations. We were not always certain we were doing the right thing. Students, for their part, experienced a range of challenges in and through workshop related to idea generation, writing practices, and social position in the classroom. I try to make these difficulties visible, name my own uncertainties, and pose questions.

Workshop Routines and Practices

How, then, was our workshop organized in practice? We relied, first, on basic routines described by classic voices and pioneers in workshop literature (Calkins, 1994; Graves, 1983)—specifically, a general three-part process that included (1) an introduction (sometimes a "minilesson" and other times informal comments), (2) open writing time (the lion's share), and (3) sharing time near the end of each session. (Calkins's [2010] more recent Units of Study curriculum suggests five possible components in a workshop session: prelude, minilesson, conferring and small-group work, mid-workshop teaching, and sharing.) Ray and Laminack (2001) assert that workshops are comprised of eight essential features: "choices about content," "time for writing," "teaching," "talking," "periods of focused study," "publication rituals," "high expectations and safety," and "structured management" (p. 15). Our workshop reflected seven of these, lacking perhaps directed "periods of focused study." Mr. Allegro did address some formal writing areas—such as persuasive writing or a specific unit on poetry—but this was often outside of the workshop. Sometimes these writing forms would subsequently show up during workshop time, but we did not explicitly teach them during the workshop. In some respects, our approach was relatively conventional and even traditional, as our primary emphasis was on alphabetic print rather than on digital, multimodal communication or the use of broader sets of materials (Kuby & Gutshall Rucker, 2015, 2016; Kuby, Gutshall Rucker, & Kirchhofer, 2015). Less conventional, however, was our commitment to flexible choice, time, and space—giving students permission to select topics, genres, purposes, as well as self-directed timelines.

This does not mean that we did not provide structure, guidance, or possible endpoints for writing practices. For example, we developed a writing process sheet—known as a blue sheet (for the paper color we printed it on)—that guided students in relation to a series of general steps as their writing progressed (see Figure 1.1). The blue sheet aimed to make writing processes (drafting, conferencing, revising, publishing) visible for young writers, emphasizing feedback and social interaction via conferencing.

Many aspects of these processes are familiar to educators, but one original feature was the opportunity for students to identify their own "investment" in a piece of writing. Typically, as part of the adult conference phase, students were asked: "How interested are you in working on [this piece of writing]?" We invited students to rate their own current writing experience from a 1 (low investment) to a 5 (high investment). The purpose was similar to the advice teachers or librarians might give to students for independent reading—that it's okay to put down a free-choice book if you don't like it, or if it's too hard for you, and to go back and find a better fit. We encouraged students to self-evaluate their writing attempts in this way, and such self-ratings helped students surface their own affective responses and guided adults in how much revision to encourage. Importantly, students were not

Figure 1.1. Writing Process Guide (Blue Sheet)

Writing Workshop
Topic or Story _____   Date   Sign

What are you working on?

STORY IDEA (think, draw, talk, read, etc.)

FIRST DRAFT—SKIP LINES!
Write up to two pages, then hold a peer conference.
Attach this sheet to your piece.

PEER CONFERENCE (before you move to your third page
or sooner)
Choose a peer.
Share your writing so far.
Complete peer conference review (on back).
Make sure your peer conference partner signs

ADULT CONFERENCE (sign up after your peer conference
is done)
Bring your writing, this sheet, and a pencil.
Rate your writing piece—how interested are you in working
on it?
1 = I feel finished with this piece now.
2 = I would like to work on it just a little more.
3 = I like this piece and want to keep working on it.
4 = I'm very interested in this piece and want to keep
developing it.
5 = I like this piece a lot. I'll keep working on it for
publication.
Continue conference on the back of form.

FINAL COPY FOR PUBLICATION
Conference process is finished, adult signs.
Type or write neatly.

OPTIONS FOR FINAL COPY
Illustrations
Dedication
Author page
Production (play, puppet show, cartoon, etc.)
Bind your final copy.

asked to self-rate writing quality—only writer investment. If investment was relatively high, students could take the work further, using peer and adult feedback to move toward a revised "final copy for publication."

The back side of the blue sheet (Figure 1.2) created space for peers and adults to record feedback, giving students a record of comments and helping adults document a student's experience, progress, and needs over time.

The blue sheet functioned as a guide and scaffold overall, and was especially valuable if students were not sure what to do next. Filling out the form itself, of course, was not the goal of workshop, and its actual use surged and faded in the classroom depending on the circumstances: It was used more consistently in the early phases of the semester or when greater support or progress tracking was needed, and less strictly later in the year or when students began to engage in sharing, feedback, and revision more independently.

We organized the classroom space for movement (Kaufmann, 2001), so students could have access to one another. Mr. Allegro's desks at first were in rows, and he gradually adjusted to pods of four desks, which created more ways to move within the classroom. We created designated spaces, such as a specific conferencing table away from the teacher's desk (although conferences tended to occur organically throughout the room). We developed an "idea station," a simple physical space near the windows, marked by a divider, with a couple of chairs, where kids could go if they were especially trying to generate writing ideas. Although students brainstormed and developed ideas throughout the classroom, this space was a way to make visible the fact that writers need room, and time, to come up with ideas. We also created an area with a range of children's books and magazines (and, after the first year, examples of student writing and publication). The hallway just outside of Mr. Allegro's room became a common space for some students or partners to work on writing ideas, as regulated by Mr. Allegro. There were two student computers in the room, which students used for online searches and information-gathering. As the workshop progressed, especially after the first year, we brought the school's laptop cart into the classroom so many students could word-process if they desired.

Mr. Allegro often began writing workshop with an idea, goal, or minilesson—sometimes briefly sharing the work of a student from a previous day, introducing a writing problem, or reading an interesting passage from a book. We did not operate with a predesigned sequence of learning goals or writing skills to instill during minilessons; instead, we tended to raise issues as they emerged. During this time, always kept brief, we encouraged discussion and used the whiteboard to draw ideas, list suggestions, and clarify norms for the day (noise level reminders and so on). Workshop itself would begin with a simple statement such as "Okay, it's time for workshop" or "Let's get started." This would switch the classroom from teacher-centered mode to a decentralized hub of student activity.

Figure 1.2. Writing Process Guide (Blue Sheet—Side 2)

Peer Conference Review

TALK TOGETHER about this piece and answer these questions: Why did the author write this piece? Does it make sense? Is it easy to read and follow? What parts of the piece are likely to catch other readers' attention?

REVIEW PARTNER WRITES—Here are some things about this piece that work well: _____

_____

_____

REVIEW PARTNER WRITES—Here is one thing that might improve the piece:

_____

_____

ADULT CONFERENCE REVIEW (remember to rate your interest in the story on the front)—Here are some things about this piece that work well:

_____

_____

_____

Here are steps to take to improve/finish this piece of writing:

Date	Steps	Adult Signs When Done

The final 10–15 minutes of workshop were devoted to public sharing of the writing that was emerging that day, usually involving audience comments, questions, and feedback. We typically invited volunteers to share pieces of their writing, and students were asked to stop their work and attend to presenting peers, although sometimes students multitasked during this time, both listening and continuing with their own writing. At other times, we encouraged non-volunteers or shy students to share their work, occasionally offering to stand with them in support or to read or show portions of their work for them, if they were open to this.

Additional contextual features of the workshop included the following:

- Each year, our workshop met for half of the year, coinciding with my second semester at the university, when my own teaching load was lighter. We would start up the workshop in January and it would go through the final weeks of school in June.
- In our first year, workshop met twice per week in the morning (9:30 A.M.) for about 60 minutes each time. In subsequent years, depending on various factors, workshop occurred either twice a week or once per week for a longer time period, such as 90–100 minutes. I was normally able to attend once per week.
- Volunteers were part of the picture. It was not uncommon to have a parent volunteer help during workshop time, which was always welcome. Occasionally, Mr. Allegro would run workshop on his own, but usually there were at least two adults in the room—Mr. Allegro and me or Mr. Allegro with a parent volunteer. Parents became important resources for us, not only in helping with conferencing but also in teaching us about kids and their histories. However, some training and preparation were important. Though parents were largely enthusiastic about the workshop, our assumptions and goals could at times conflict with a volunteer's expectation. As the workshop became known in the school, other observers (teachers, other parents, and/or education students from my department) would come to observe and sometimes help.
- We experienced flexible oversight from administrators. Two different principals worked in Mr. Allegro's building during the 5 years I was there, and both showed curiosity about what we were doing and exhibited little tendency or pressure to actively regulate things. They were, if anything, pleased that someone from the local university was showing interest in the school and happy to see active writing. The local district was placing intense focus on reading scores, using highly structured curricula at the elementary level. The flipside was that the writing curriculum was given comparatively less regulatory attention. State tests, however, were given at the 4th-grade level, and writing was a component of the state test. This was a concern for Mr.

Allegro, and he tried to keep track of the content and support that students would need to be successful on the test, administered each year in April.

- Behind all this, Mr. Allegro and I found that we were compatible in the classroom together. He saw me as an interested parent and community member, and we were able to work together with relative ease and confidence. Working in Mr. Allegro's classroom was something I looked forward to each week.

CONTEXT: REFLECTING ON RACE AND CLASS

The city where Mr. Allegro and I work is largely identified as a blue-collar town, though this story takes place in a school of relative socioeconomic privilege within the city. Adams Elementary is a middle-class, majority White school with about 350 students. Demographically, roughly 85% of the student population was identified as White at the time I was there, and 12–14% received free or reduced-price lunch. This contrasted with the school district at large, which was roughly 51% White and where over 50% of students received free or reduced-price lunch.

The city and school district overall comprise diverse cultures, languages, and communities—including African American, European American, Latino, Native American, and Southeast Asian—yet significant de facto race segregation continues to define the experiences of many students.

Critical sociocultural theory calls us to account for "how learning and teaching both influence and are influenced by power relations" and how literacy "involves the appropriation of ideologies of language" (Handsfield, 2016, p. 89; see also Gee, 2001). It resists color-blind and "context neutral" assumptions (Milner, 2010), highlighting specific affordances of race, class, and gender. For example, the flexible administrative control we experienced at Adams reflected privilege, as administrators expected students to do relatively well on tests, and test scores correlated with race and class demographics across the city. Adults and students alike at Adams were, consequently, offered greater trust and autonomy in their own learning. Increased volunteer participation was also evident, understood here not as a difference in parent engagement or interest in different parts of the city, but more as a product of class. Higher family income generated greater resources and flexibility to participate in school, in addition to a general sense of confidence, entitlement, and comfort among adults about being within the school setting itself.

English language learners were present at Adams, yet as a small minority. Standard English was assumed in all classroom interactions. Nonstandard uses of English often raise questions or fears among teachers about the forms of language that are most appropriate and needed for "success" in school—and about how much teacher control, direction, and correction are necessary to prepare students for the "real world." Students from minoritized communities often receive socially mediated, negative messaging or micro-aggressions (Suárez-Orozco et al., 2015) in relation to their home languages and/or uses of English—messages that erode trust and confidence in taking risks with written language in school. As members of an historically privileged community, adults and students alike at Adams Elementary seldom experienced such challenges, and thus possibilities for "experimentation" with writing, as well as some forms of writer confidence, were more easily assumed than in other schools in the district—although, as we will see, challenges with confidence at Adams were still an issue.

These realities do not suggest, however, that flexibility and experimentation are not possible or desirable with a wider range of children and specifically in more culturally or socioeconomically diverse school settings. Indeed, research on English language learners reminds us that writing development is highly idiosyncratic, recursive in nature, and that new language learners benefit from authentic, self-sponsored forms of writing within environments that allow for flexibility, choice, and significant risk-taking (Samway, 2006). The point, rather, is that we cannot take any context, nor one's own cultural perspective, for granted—and each setting requires conscious attention to sociocultural dimensions as they interact with privilege and power. Workshop experiences are altered by specific school contexts, by valuations of particular languages, and by the daily experiences of the students who speak them. Samway (2006) describes, for example, how teachers in a 5th-grade writing workshop for bilingual learners shifted from a more open-choice context to one emphasizing a "memoir unit of study," especially after considering the increasing marginalization of their learners in a state where bilingual education was under direct attack. These teachers felt that the memoir unit was a particularly important and motivating opportunity for their students to talk and write about their lives, histories, and native languages in school. As we weigh issues of how much "structure" and "direction" to give a workshop, or to writing instruction generally, perhaps the deepest question is not whether there should be "more or less" structure, but rather where the structure comes from—whose structure and whose needs and purposes are driving the direction we give.

Having a strong lens for student agency is thus central to a critical sociocultural approach, and to my own descriptions in the chapters that follow. Such a lens seeks ways for teachers and students to maneuver within ideologically and economically driven systems. Dyson (1997, 2003, 2013) shows us how even in relatively controlled and traditional writing contexts, young children actively negotiate language and power, regularly repurposing the "official" intentions of the adult systems around them. Handsfield (2016) asserts that we must view teachers and students "as both consumers and agents of curriculum with the ability, or power, to creatively appropriate curricula and Discourses of language and literacy" (p. 91). Such a stance asks us: How willing are we to see beyond official curricular intentions? How open are we to the ways in which children actively engage systems of power and signification around them as they experiment with and take on new forms of language?

As this work unfolds within a largely White, middle-class setting, I seek to decenter dominant or prevailing viewpoints, including at times my own, and especially those predicated on the centrality of writing products or endpoints. I often give emphasis to writing experiences on the margins, to students who otherwise might be seen as struggling or "below standard." It was not difficult to find such experiences in Mr. Allegro's classroom, and I write generously about such students not to romanticize but to explore student agency. This takes my focus "into the moment" of specific encounters—to see what possibilities exist as students respond to, and act on, their environment, engaging the languages, powers, and relationships around them. My hope is that readers will join me in recognizing that the events at Adams Elementary, though not generalizing automatically to other schools or classrooms, may nevertheless lead to various resonances, stirrings, partial recognitions, and even productive differences by which we can always learn from another's practice.

KEEPING ALIVE A LISTENING STANCE
WITH UPPER ELEMENTARY STUDENTS

In this opening chapter, I've highlighted the notions of learning as participation, and writing as play and exploration, to clarify the instructional decisions we made in designing our writers' workshop for 4th-graders. These theoretical concepts reinforce the instinct Mr. Allegro and I shared—that is, not to emphasize writing endpoints and "expectations" as much as ongoing interactions and student engagement in the moment. Such a stance felt risky, but also relevant to our current moment in education, where learning to read and write in schools tends to be controlled and dominated by market forces (Altwerger, 2005; Rose, 2014) and by a technical rationality that privileges discrete skills, quantifiable outcomes, and "world-class standards." Boldt (2009) laments that "space for young people to use materials, social relations, and time in the classroom for anything other than predetermined academic outcomes—in other words, the time to play with ideas, materials, and one another—has largely disappeared" (p. 12). In such a context, we need vision and tools to resist simplistic framings of young people and their literacies, to generate possibilities, images, and models that keep our thinking and practice agile. Teachers need new vocabularies to validate and nurture ongoing observations and instincts about how children learn and what they might need, especially when those observations and instincts do not match a given curriculum and bureaucratic or market-driven assumptions.

Workshop observers and advocates, however, rightfully caution against simplistic views of flexibility and naïve versions of being "student-centered." They call for conscientious, active interventions on the part of adults—sometimes in terms of engaging classroom power, privilege, and politics, and other times in terms of greater attention to standards and clear uses of expertise to support academic growth. Lensmire (1994), describing his own experience teaching in a 3rd-grade writing workshop, criticizes the romantic rhetoric around workshop models, noting how social boundaries and student power dynamics permeated the workshop space; he calls for a more conscientious teacher role in shaping classroom community. Scholars like Delpit (1988, 1995/2006) have long reminded us that progressive, "student-centered" contexts for literacy are not culturally or politically neutral. Rather, without critical cultural awareness, they perform a sort of progressive blindness, favoring those who are already connected to languages of power and privilege. Students whose language practices are marginalized in the larger society need explicit ways to learn codes of power: They must be "taught." Atwell (1998), in a revised version of her landmark work *In the Middle*, refers to teaching "with a capital T" in workshop—encouraging an "interventionist" mindset, reminding teachers to forward their expertise as needed, to make expectations crystal clear. An increased "interventionist" stance is seen in the recent work of Calkins and colleagues (Calkins, 2010; Calkins, Ehrenworth, & Lehman, 2012; Calkins, Hartman, White, & Units of Study Coauthors, 2003), as teachers are offered explicit structures, tools, directions, and even wording for how to run a workshop and for supporting students in reaching specific standards.

I do not disagree with or seek to refute such critiques, orientations, and reminders. As Dewey (1938) reminded us long ago, teaching is not about stepping back to observe kids as they learn on their own. The risk I point to in drawing attention to the theories above—to notions of "learning as participation" and "writing as play and exploration"—is our increasing tendency to miss the child and the complexity of a child's learning interaction—that is, to focus singularly on what kids "should" be learning and how, while losing a sense of learners' starting points, what their own initiatives and purposes are, and how writing might function with and among children themselves. What I aim to make distinct in this work is leaning into and keeping alive a listening stance with upper elementary students in an era when adults are asked to turn, sometimes exclusively, toward standards and assessment. We live and teach in an accountability era where educators' fundamental work of listening to children, of seeing and respecting children's modes of communication and learning, is hard to sustain. I hope to offer educators, in the words of Boldt (2009), "access to a language that competes with current utilitarian demands" and that can support teachers "to take a principled stance on the value of creativity . . . including writing as play" (p. 17). We need ways to revisit and reassess common assumptions about what it means to learn to write, what writing is for, and how upper elementary students, as children, might choose to engage in purposeful communication with others and for themselves.

CHAPTER 2

Writing as Visualizing Popular Worlds

In my own teacher preparation, writing was typically divided into three general forms—narrative, descriptive, and persuasive—and narrative, especially "personal narrative," was considered the best starting point for helping writers gain confidence. Writing about the self, the assumption goes, is easier, more accessible, and motivating; writers draws directly from what they know in generating material; one can narrate a story as it was experienced, from memory. For example, a popular book on children's writing workshops (Fletcher & Portalupi, 2001) suggests that teachers initially model writer thinking by "sharing two or three personal stories from your own life" (p. 37), offering various prompts if students get stuck: Do you play sports? What about other activities like dance or chess? Who's your best friend or a good friend? Ever go to the hospital? The prompts direct writers to various hobbies, relationships, and memorable life experiences—and imply, at least indirectly, that personal narrative is a natural genre for young writers. In effect, such prompts say: "Just write about something you experienced—tell it as it happened."

As our workshop developed, we noticed different patterns. Personal narrative, writing about the self and one's own experiences, appeared less compelling to many 4th-graders. Certainly, students' sources for writing, as constructivist theory would suggest, reflected lived experience in some way. Yet, when students were given space and freedom to write, the shape of that lived experience often reflected media-generated, popular worlds—video games they played, children's book series, movie plot lines, superheroes, and TV characters they liked (Dyson, 1997, 2003). Our students, it turned out, were less likely to dwell on "realistic" personal experiences and far more compelled to represent and actively filter various "mediascapes" (Attalah & Shade, 2006; Newkirk, 2001), shaping their own voices and language in relation to the virtual worlds and multiple literacies around them.

Such impulses placed the visual imagination into the nucleus of our writing workshop, and for some students, especially those most challenged by writing in conventional forms, the act of visualizing popular worlds became a crucial foothold. These students used drawing and visual imagery not merely to "illustrate" their existing work, but to realize, imagine, and activate what they wanted and needed to say. In these cases, visual representation created a symbolic meaning-world from which writing confidence, identity, purpose, and ideas could develop over time. Though drawing is considered essential for the development of early childhood and primary school writers (Clay, 1975; Emig, 1983), we found that visualized, multimodal communication continued to be crucial for many upper elementary students, shaping fundamental perceptions of text, communication, and writing.

This insight ran contrary to several common assumptions. For example, as teachers we may resist student writing that focuses on popular culture—video games or movies—believing that these are distracting or not appropriate topics for school writing. Mr. Allegro told me he had felt this way himself early on, as a few students began to write about a popular kids' TV show, *SpongeBob SquarePants*. Adults also might assume that "real" writing looks a particular way—for example, as first-person, realistic stories done in neat handwriting, or as objective, expository essays that occur in consecutive lines of printed text. Teachers and parents may further believe that upper elementary learners should have grown out of the need to draw—and that visual impulses, if they occur, should only be allowed *after* actual writing has been completed rather than as a central part of idea generation and writer thinking.

From a theoretical perspective, Gee (2001) argues that there is no pure standard of "literacy" from a linguistic point of view, but instead multiple literacies that apply to specific sociocultural situations. Students, however, typically internalize school-sanctioned literacy as "normal" or "correct," even when those norms fail to reflect their needs or the ways they engage multiple literacies in their daily lives (Alvermann, 2004; Li, 2008; Moje et al., 2004; Nieto, 2002). Such students are at risk of seeing their own ways with language as deficient. This chapter suggests the ways in which a writing community might shift what counts as literate practice, especially as students are encouraged to perceive writing as connected to meaningful realities (virtual or actual) in their lives. Below, I share three narrative cases from our first year of writing workshop. In each case, I profile a student who struggled to compose in conventional, academic forms, and whose writing fell outside what we initially expected students to produce. Given space, choice, and time to locate their interests, these students relied heavily on popular media forms, as well as their own visual imagination, to shape what they wanted to say and to create a meaningful space for communication. In each case, their unconventional writing helped us see "where they were" and "what they needed to do" as writers.

MARTIN: SCREEN SHOTS AND VIDEO GAMES

March 14, Year 1: I head off to find Martin, a 4th-grader in Mr. Allegro's class who appears to struggle with traditional academic tasks. Yesterday, I observed his complete involvement in yet another detailed drawing of a video game. He did no formal writing. Martin is a fascinating case for writers' workshop. He taps his imagination by meticulously drawing virtual worlds in his notebook—sketching castles, traps, dragons, and staircases, the various obstacles that his video game protagonists must overcome. So far, he has created elaborate drawings from various "Super Mario" games—the virtual worlds of the characters Mario and Luigi. Yet, Martin isn't inclined to put this mental life into words on paper. Martin has an individual education plan (IEP); the physical act of writing out words and sentences is a struggle for him. He grasps his pencil awkwardly, and letters come laboriously. In many ways, Martin can tell so much more by drawing.

It took us a while to figure out what Martin, in fact, was doing in writers' workshop. He was among the most intent of students—choosing initially not to partner with anyone, though he was completely immersed at his desk, hunched over his paper, actively composing, drawing with rather extraordinary detail. Over time, we realized that Martin's very notions of story, and of writing, were fully interconnected with computer screens and gaming (Figure 2.1). We could see, for example, that Martin's "texts" amounted to screen shots, video screens themselves, and that Martin's "stories" re-created the quests of various video game heroes—those who face a series of obstacles (monsters, dropoffs, and convoluted pathways) to achieve various "levels" of completion. Often, such protagonists must locate certain tools or keys that give them access to new levels (Figure 2.2).

No adult working with Martin during workshop left without a sense of fascination and respect for his remarkable drawings, attention to detail, and rich engagement. We also faced the question: "What *is* writing?" Martin was fully engaged, using the tools at his disposal to re-create detailed worlds that he found meaningful, almost as if he were a musician composing a score that was playing in his head. But what about conventional words, sentences, and paragraphs? As one adult volunteer put it: "Shouldn't he be actually writing?" We all faced this concern in some way, and we worked to find an appropriate response, a way that would simultaneously honor Martin's existing work while encouraging his continued literacy development. We emphasized to ourselves that Martin *was* writing—and, as was evident in his investment and energy, he seemed to be doing exactly what he needed to do to learn and stay engaged. We felt that Martin was striving to communicate in a domain of confidence but also finding the edge of his abilities. Martin, we believed further, was establishing for himself a meaningful, symbolic world of representation—a written display outside of himself—from

Figure 2.1. Examples of Martin's Video Game Drawings in Class

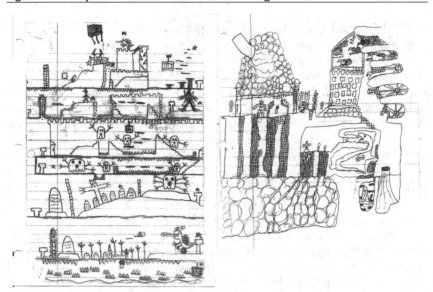

which he would eventually generate language in new forms. In other words, Martin's writing development would not proceed by putting *away* his video game drawings, but instead would occur *through* them—particularly in relationship to oral language production and with targeted support.

To support Martin's writing growth, we made active efforts to spark conversation with him about his work, a common prompt being: "Tell me about this part, Martin. . . ." Martin talked openly about his drawings and seemed to appreciate his role as an expert in such interactions. To help Martin experience his own language in written form, an adult (sometimes one of us, sometimes a volunteer) would, at times, write out his oral language on paper as he spoke. For example, one dictated excerpt, based on a detailed drawing, reads:

> King Bowzer locked Luigi in a cage high up in the air. Then Mario comes to the basement and finds the door. Mario opens the door and goes inside. Then Mario finds his weapons lying on the ground. He picked up the weapons. Mario then found a tube and jumped inside of it. . . . He also found a cannon and a hill with spikes on it and a monster at the top of the hill. So Mario jumped in the cannon and blasted off to fight the monster. . . .

Martin's recorded language, as evident here, reflects the imperatives of the video game—a simple plot, a series of adventures (then . . . then . . .

Figure 2.2. Example of Martin's Video Game Drawing

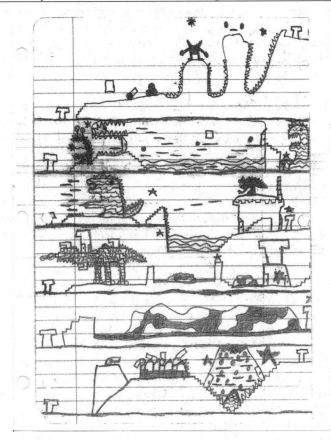

then . . .), various levels of challenge, with the end goal being to defeat a nemesis and/or locate some treasure. Simple action carries the day. We used such adult-transcribed texts to read aloud back to Martin, so he could hear his own "voice" and "writing." Mr. Allegro or a volunteer might stop after transcribing a few lines of Martin's language and say: "Let me read this back to you, Martin"—and then, after reading it would ask: "How did that sound, Martin?"

Such interactions and support revealed our own lingering concerns with "endpoints," with getting Martin "somewhere" in his writing. We wanted to honor and observe Martin's own unique emergence as a writer, yet we also wanted to help him write conventionally. Indeed, Martin gradually built a relationship between his own visual imagination, oral language, and conventional writing. Over time, he started incorporating words onto his pages—sometimes just labeling items in a picture, occasionally inserting snippets of dialogue. In many ways, reflecting the development of an early writer, Martin began to create meaningful links and relationships between images and words (Clay, 1975; Meier, 2011). In Figures 2.3 and 2.4, for example, we see many of Martin's strengths as a writer. The drawings reflect his attention to detail and his ability to visually depict a place he knows well.

With the drawing in place, Martin attempts language labels—naming "water towers," "briges" (bridges), "a dowm" (dome), a "hows" (house), and a park. He begins to insert dialogue to reflect a conflict in the video game plot: "You will pay," "diy" (die), "Mom," and "diy monstors" (die monsters). Here, Martin shows us distinct things about his learning zone—namely, that his motivation to use language stems from locating an area of expertise, a place of confidence from which he has things to say. For Martin, this is connected to video game experiences, which have a complex visual dimension. Martin also needs space and flexibility to experiment with modes of communication that work for him. For him, integrating a visual setting with bits of writing seems productive; his visual representations form a basis from which conventional language becomes purposeful.

Building from Martin's Images

When I sit down next to Martin, he informs me that his most recent drawing world is called Gex. "I play Gex I and Gex III. I'm almost to the wrestling level," he says. I overhear Vanni, who is reading a story from one of his classmates, saying, "Dang. This story is long!" Madeline is next to us, reviewing her recent publication. She shows me her dedication page: "I've dedicated my book to Alana," she says, referring to her friend seated nearby. Martin sits patiently as these interactions occur around him.

My goal today is to build upon Martin's growth and help him share more about his video worlds in words and sentences.

> "What is Gex?" I ask.
> "He's a lizard."
> "Is he like a gecko?"
> "Yes."

I ask Martin to tell me about his Gex drawing, and he goes through its various parts. He describes sand monsters, a mummy, portals, and a sun that has been covered over.

"What can you tell me about Gex?"

"Well, he walks on two legs and he whacks his tail. And the only way to kill the sand monsters is to get the cover off of the sun—and then they turn to cement."

Once again, I am struck by how Martin's story thinking is shaped by both video game content and format. He thinks less about storyline or plot

Figure 2.3. Martin's Drawing with Labels Incorporated

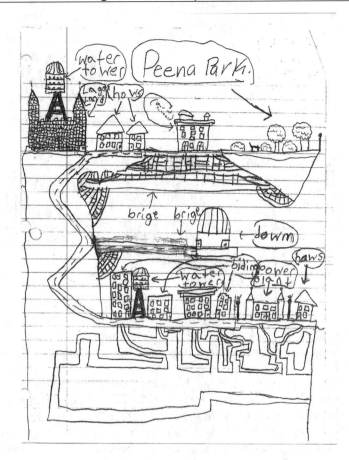

as I conceive them and more about video game screens as texts and the nature of obstacles that must be overcome. He is so engrossed that I wonder how I might help him see links between his gaming imagination and conventional writing. I take out a sheet and put the word *Gex* in the middle inside a small circle, then draw several lines reaching out in spider-legs fashion—a simple prewriting or brainstorming format. "What are some things you want people to know about Gex?"

My spider web format is a break with how Martin conceives his work. I can feel it. Martin's energy flow seems to be interrupted. Is this a useful moment, opening up Martin's writing world a bit? Or am I detracting from his process—not understanding where he's at? I live with this tension, hoping to help Martin prioritize a few selected pieces for written communication. To my relief he offers ideas, which I take down on the paper. I record a section on "how the sun got covered up," then on "the mummy," then on

Figure 2.4. Martin's Drawing with Dialogue Incorporated

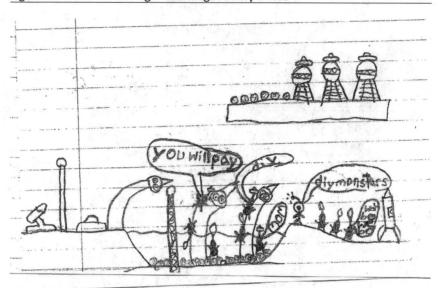

"the portals," and then on "the sand monsters." Because Gex is the hero or central character, I ask Martin what people should know about Gex. He gives me some detail: Gex is purple and green, has two arms, stands on two legs, and is "cool."

We refer to Martin's drawings throughout the conversation. As we talk about the portals, Martin says that each one leads into a different time zone. One portal leads to a time before the dinosaurs; another takes you into space. There are four portals, and we decide to number them so we will remember what each one does. I record the numbers on Martin's drawing. After a few minutes, I ask, "How should we start writing?" But I quickly sense that the question is too abstract and rooted in my own needs. I try another approach: "Who should hear about Gex? As you share your work, who do you want to tell this to?" Martin decides that Mr. Allegro and his class will be his audience. Then we decide where to start. We look at the spider legs on our planning sheet. Martin decides he'd like his classmates and teacher first to learn about who Gex is, after which we'll tell them about the portals.

To generate text, I write out what Martin says about Gex, using *cloze* spaces. That is, every few words or so, I leave out a word and just put an underscore line in the blank space. For example: "Gex is 4 feet 10 _____ just like _____. Gex is _____." This scaffold encourages Martin to reread his own thinking in print and also to begin to supply and compose a few words on his own. I write out just over a page of Martin's language, leaving about a dozen words out as I go. We then partner-read the page together aloud, and I encourage Martin to supply the missing words orally as we go: "Gex is 4 feet 10 <u>inches</u> just like <u>me</u>. Gex is <u>cool</u>." Next, I invite Martin to read the page on his own and to use his own handwriting to fill in the blanks. He knows the story well. He reads and writes intently as I step away.

Learning from Martin

Given different circumstances, or a deficit view of his abilities, Martin could have been pulled out or excluded from the classroom space. By contrast, a choice-oriented workshop helped Martin reveal how he thinks, what he cares about, and his remarkable talent for drawing virtual worlds. His participation in a community of writers also mattered, especially one in which sharing a range of writing forms was acceptable. This allowed Martin to act as a full writing member, to locate an area of expertise, and to gain the confidence he needed to take new steps with language. Indeed, as weeks went by, Martin began to try stories with increasing language—hybrid texts with intermixed words and pictures. Such writings (see Figure 2.5) continued to focus on video game worlds, virtual characters, and simple action-oriented plots.

In these kinds of writings, Martin continued to rely on drawings to anchor his writing, yet he now ventured to turn video screen action into prose—to tell a story in his own words. His writing reveals a sense of narrative sequence, a story grammar that includes conflict and resolution, and the development of conventional spellings. The visual, which reflects the story action carefully, is scaled to provide balance between drawing and prose.

We learned a great deal from Martin. We realized, for example, that our job was not simply to step back and leave Martin on his own; it involved careful observation and key decisions—suspending, at times, our impulse to push Martin to write like other kids—and helping, at other times, to convert his ideas into print. In terms of specific strategies, dictation offered Martin a chance to experience his own language meaningfully in written code. The modified strategy of dictating Martin's oral language using cloze spaces was a turning point, allowing him to *produce* familiar, self-determined language meaningfully—blending speaking, reading, and writing—in ways that were not overwhelming. Most fundamentally, our work involved taking a stance toward Martin that saw purposeful literacy in his drawings and that engaged him on his own terms. Flexibility in our notion of "story" was essential—a willingness to listen and understand how a video screen tells a story, and how and why this might matter to Martin, both personally and in terms of literacy development.

CARLA: AUTHOR-ARTIST IN COMMUNITY

This second case demonstrates how Carla, a 4th-grader new to the school that year, used the flexible norms of our workshop to navigate a learning

Figure 2.5. Martin's Writing, Later in Workshop (Edited Language Below)

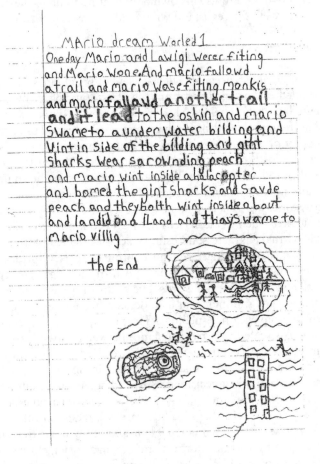

Mario Dream World 1

One day Mario and Luigi were fighting and Mario won. Mario followed a trail and Mario was fighting monkeys and Mario followed another trail and it led to the ocean and Mario swam to an underwater building and giant sharks were surrounding the beach. Mario went inside a helicopter and bombed the giant sharks and saved the beach, and they both went inside a boat and landed on an island. And they swam to Mario's village. The end.

space between her artistic strengths, the risks she experienced in writing conventionally, and a sense of social purpose in the classroom.

May 22, Year 1: Today, Carla shows me a series of drawings she's been working on for several sessions. She has been highly motivated to draw images lately, which once again has raised uncertainty among the adults during workshop: How much should workshop in 4th grade be about "writing" in a traditional sense? To what extent are Carla's images valuable in their own right? Is she learning the skills she needs when she is just drawing and not writing? Different from Martin, Carla has already completed a few written pieces. Her first was called "The Magic Book," which reminded me of the story *Jumanji* (Van Allsburg, 1981), as it plunged its characters magically into unexpected and chaotic events. She has also written a piece called "The White Witch." In my notes partway through the term, I've noted that Carla is "imaginative" in her thinking and that she can write with a "vibrant" voice. For growth, I've recorded that her writing could use more focus—it tends to scatter a bit. Carla's writing exhibits a great number of misspellings.

Visual images appear to be Carla's real love, and often, like Martin, she will go for periods of time not "writing" anything as she pursues her work intently. For a few weeks in the middle of the term, she alternated her workshop days between drawing pictures and, with a push from adults, writing conventionally in prose. Yet, Carla has come up with another solution to the pull between writing and drawing. She has decided to create a short book of drawings, using the backside of each image she draws to write out story-starter sentences. The idea came from a book available in Mr. Allegro's classroom, *The Mysteries of Harris Burdick* (Van Allsburg, 1984), which uses captivating, full-page images along with concise, provocative phrases to activate readers' imaginations. Carla lets me know that she wants her book to spark her classmates' imaginations—and that it might help her peers come up with their own story ideas for writing. In fact, over the course of several sessions working on her own, Carla now has an entire collection of scenes—one section drawn in color and one in black and white. She calls the collection "The Idea Book," and her original sketches include a giant ice cream sundae, a sunset over a town and mountains, a young person getting rained on *under* an umbrella, a girl with binoculars looking at fairies under a leaf, and more.

We go through each drawing, and Carla reads her story-starter sentences aloud. For her drawing of fairies (Figure 2.6), Carla's story starter is "Wow look Fairy are real and there eating a feast." On this page, Carla points out that the picture is made from the fairies' perspective—thus, the leaf and bush look large in comparison, whereas the language of the written prompt takes the perspective of the human observer depicted in the scene. The drawing is rich in perspective, imagination, and playfulness.

Figure 2.6. Carla's Drawing of Fairies

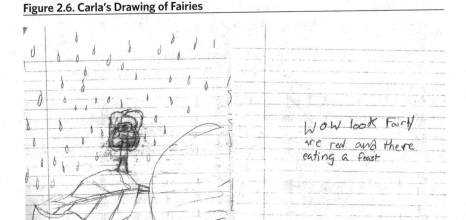

Another image (Figure 2.7) offers a close-up of three hummingbirds feeding on flowers, with the starter sentence: "We better get some food or else we will . . ." Carla's drawings show an affinity for the natural world; she has skillfully drawn birds in different flight positions, providing perspective to show one bird and bush at a distance. She creatively personifies the birds, taking their perspective with an imaginative prompt—using the phrase to infuse the scene with urgency and to offer possible directions for writing.

After these images, at the end of the book, Carla has created an interactive page, where she invites readers to list pictures they enjoyed. It's titled "Pictures you like?" and has lines where readers can write down a favorite image. At the bottom of the page, Carla has included an encouraging phrase: "Put your mind to it. See!"

Offering Feedback

As we finish reading the book, I tell Carla how impressed I am. She indicates that she wants to publish this work, so I begin to give some written feedback on loose paper, because we've run out of blue sheets. I write first, "A lovely book, Carla!" I hope to reinforce her visual sense, emphasis on creativity and imagination, perspective-taking, and awareness of audience—especially in creating a book explicitly for other young writers. Validation is called for, even as I wonder: Am I being rigorous enough? Should Carla be asked to

Figure 2.7. Carla's Hummingbird Page

We better get some food or else we will . . .

write more than a series of single sentences? Is she learning to write in ways that will be valued as she heads toward middle school?

Despite such questions, I'm not inclined to give critical messages at this point. My stance stems from several observations: "The Idea Book" goes well beyond any form of robotic or perfunctory writing on Carla's part. Instead, she is fully invested. Carla integrates acts of reading and writing with this project, as she develops a book that will support the writing of others. She has real audiences in mind, and her work will immediately benefit other student writers in the class and perhaps be enjoyed by future 4th-graders. Perhaps most important, Carla is nurturing a positive, though still fragile, writer identity. Carla realizes that her writing conventions, especially her spelling, often do not conform to formal expectations. Writing is a risky business for her. She is vulnerable to being judged by peers and adults based on surface features. In addition, as a new student at the school this year, Carla is still managing social relationships and her place in the 4th grade, striving to build connections and friendships. For these reasons, supporting and validating Carla's emergent and creative writing strikes me as especially important.

In adult conferences, according to our blue sheet process (see Chapter 1), rating one's writing a "5" (the highest rating students can give for their investment in a piece of writing) entails substantive feedback and attempts at revision, often followed by publication. Carla has given this work a 5.

To finalize Carla's work, I decide to keep my growth comments simple and to gently focus on editing her prompts. We look again at her spelling and whether readers will be able to make sense of the story starters. When I come across a word that's misspelled, I underline it in pencil and write the correct spelling on the feedback page I've started. Some might fear that I'm making things too easy for Carla—that she should figure out such spellings on her own or be given strategies and resources to do so independently. My concern is that, for this writer, "sounding" out words will likely lead to further mistakes and frustration, and looking up words will quickly become busywork and may even feel like punishment. Carla has worked thoughtfully on this piece, has risked something original, and I don't want such impressions to land on her now.

I ask Carla to go back through her piece and make corrections with a pencil and eraser, using the spellings I've offered. Our spelling list has increased to about 10 words, which does not include every misspelling I can see. Carla reveals to me, as she gets started, that her dad usually circles her misspelled words in red, and she has to write everything over again—to start over. Our process leads Carla to self-correct a few words, like changing "whin" to *when*. As she does so, she pauses and apologizes: "I'm sorry. I'm a really bad speller." We talk about a few patterns: for example, that *ice cream* and *feast* are spelled with /ea/ and not just /e/ to make the long *e* sound. I let her go back to her desk. Her job is to make the corrections and cut off a few ragged edges on her paper so the book will be ready to publish. I can see how, for this imaginative 4th-grader, overemphasis on surface errors, especially early in the process, might turn her away from writing altogether.

Carla's Creative Pathway

In what ways has Carla made her constructive learning visible? To what extent is visualized multimodal communication essential to her development? In "The Idea Book," Carla makes the most of her visual talents, depicting creative scenes and using lines skillfully to make creative shapes and show perspective. Such scenes incorporate concise bursts of written language in the service of her peers and their writing. Her booklet exhibits skills essential to the writer's craft. It is exceptionally audience-centered. Her drawings are fundamentally interactive, carefully designed to elicit a response. She explicitly invites feedback from readers. Carla maneuvers with ease between various perspectives—taking up the voice of characters in her images, even as she designs the work around the needs of others. She has modeled her work on a popular children's book, tweaking the "story-starter" concept to make it her own. The investment that Carla shows in this work, moreover, creates a foundation for initial attention to conventional writing elements—in this case, accurate spellings—so readers can get the most from her book. As she has revealed, this is a personally sensitive area.

Flexible workshop norms give Carla the space to showcase her talents, manage risk, and find social purpose to her writing. Visually oriented writing, for instance, helps Carla negotiate varying purposes. She connects with a children's book she has enjoyed, remaking it for herself and her peers. She takes up the position of an author-artist, experimenting with a nontraditional form. The author-artist role allows Carla to engage the visual sphere while also helping her meet classroom expectations to "write." Realizing that her skills with conventions like spelling leave her vulnerable, Carla steers a creative pathway—one where she can simultaneously contribute in workshop and perhaps minimize the ever-present potential for damage to her self-confidence. As a student seeking and building new social relationships, Carla's writing reaches out to others, providing peers with a sourcebook and tool. Her final page invites others to actively speak back to her, to assess her work and give validation. Different from Martin, she writes explicitly with others' experiences and needs in mind, seeming to seek relationship.

Such observations help adults see what Carla might need in the way of support. Flexible norms have allowed her to act purposefully, resolve tensions, and assert agency as she crafts a way to engage in literate practice. From this position, she needs validation for her creative navigations as well as feedback that generously supports her desire to write for peers. Surface conventions should not consume our attention—or if they do, only once Carla has first experienced her writing as respected and purposeful in the community. Carla certainly benefited, at times, from the adult expectation that she should write only with words and sentences, which she was willing to do. Yet most important seemed to be a degree of flexibility, especially in light of a precarious writer identity, for Carla to find her own way.

RICKY: LEARNING TO WRITE AS PLAY

This third case illuminates the work of a student who, to find motivation and an appropriate literacy challenge, interweaves multiple popular sources to tell a story. Even as the year comes to an end, Ricky, a wiry 4th-grader with bright blond hair, relies largely on visual imagination to sustain and drive his attempts to think and write narratively.

June 5, Year 1: I sit next to Ricky, and I see that he has "Archie the Turtle" out, a story Ricky is writing much like a comic book, with several blocked pictures and very few words. Last week, I noted that Ricky's work with "Archie" was taking off. In comparison to some of our most confident writers in class, Ricky's independent writing output has been limited. He partners actively with peers, loves to listen to stories, and contributes ideas during sharing sessions. Composing his own thoughts on paper has been more difficult. Ricky, like Martin, is a good example of a student for whom participating in and around a community of learners seems essential—where active engagement and social relationships, along with adult input and support, lead gradually to efforts to use language in new ways. This has required patience and trust on our part.

The fact that many of Ricky's friends have published stories, and that it is near the end of the year, seems now to be particularly motivating for him. He is working hard to put together "Archie the Turtle" on his own, and, like both Martin and Carla, is writing in a way that seems to work for him. The cartoon genre limits the need for words and sentences, and, in a way, matches Ricky's personality: It is visual, witty, and playful. Archie's world is alive with images of starfish, evil sea creatures, and humorous insertions like a "Sea Needle" (a mock Space Needle). At the top of each page, Ricky typically composes a sentence or two to forward his narrative. For example, his first page opens with a dramatic header (see Figure 2.8): "One day in the middle of the Pacific terror struck the heart of millions"—a sentence that foreshadows drama and sensationalizes, similar to a movie trailer. The rest of the page is a series of cartoonish scenes relating a story sequence with minimal words. As with Martin and Carla, the visual dimension seems to support Ricky's ability to connect with his own story, to see and experience what's happening, and to integrate it gradually with language.

Thinking from a Reader's Perspective

As I sit next to Ricky, I ask about his progress. He says he wants to finish the page he's on (page two), but isn't sure what to write next. I can see he hasn't advanced very far from where he was last week, as a big battle was looming between Archie the Turtle and his archenemy, Pufferfish. Ricky tells me he actually knows what he *wants* to happen—that the two enemies become "sidekicks" and work together—but he's not sure how to get to this resolution. We decide to go over to the idea station to talk about ideas. Once situated, Ricky reiterates his plan that Pufferfish will become "good" and end up working with Archie the Turtle. I tell Ricky that when I try to move a story forward, I often go back and just reread what I've written already to give me some momentum. Ricky says he does that, too, and I invite him to read from page one.

As Ricky reads, I inquire about his cartoon drawings: "So, what's happening here?" For each image, Ricky can tell me right away what's going on, but this is far less clear to a reader, so we begin to discuss what Ricky knows, what he wants his reader to know, and what the reader can probably tell so far. Ricky connects with this process and even offers up his own analogy.

"It's like an artist," he says. "When they paint something, but you can't tell what it is, and they might put a label on the bottom for what's happening."

Figure 2.8. Ricky's Story—Title Page and Page One (with Dialogue and Labels)

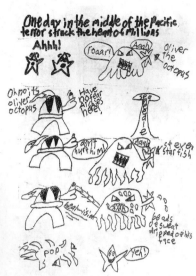

I say, "Yeah, that's an example." We talk briefly about how sometimes an artist uses such a label, and other times the artist might want the observer to speculate.

Ricky says with a wry expression: "Sometimes an artist might just throw ink on paper, and you can't tell if it's supposed to be water or what."

We work through the cartoon images on page one, which at this point has just a few speech bubbles with dialogue. I stop to say that I can't tell what the creature is near the top of the page. Ricky says it's an octopus, and I offer a few ways he can signal this to the reader. Perhaps Archie can say in the speech bubble: "Stop right there, Octopus!"—or Ricky can just use a label in the margin, "Dangerous Octopus," with an arrow pointing to the creature. Ricky says he wants to try both and see which he likes. He decides he wants to use an alliterative name: "Oliver Octopus." As we talk, Ricky shares that he has Captain Underpants books at home that use labels like this, a revelation that helps me see a relationship between his reading and writing—and to understand the popular genre that is likely informing his work. In the end, Ricky decides he likes both additions to the story, and we go to another frame. We next discuss whether the starfish in Oliver's hand is being held hostage or not, which leads to a brief discussion of what a hostage is. Inquiring into the details of Ricky's visuals—taking the images seriously and asking a few inferential questions (Is the starfish being taken hostage or just being held?)—helps Ricky engage the logic of his own work and consider ways to advance the story.

Figure 2.9. Ricky's Story—Pages Two and Three

Ricky seems to understand the work we are doing—namely, to think from a reader's perspective and to provide clues to help readers make sense of the story. On page one, he decides to draw beads of sweat on Oliver Octopus to show how Archie's heat vision is burning him, and then writes "beads of sweat" in the cartoon margin with an arrow—writing techniques very common in Captain Underpants. He revises one of his speech bubbles on his own, on page two (see Figure 2.9), with new reader-centered awareness. Where Archie says: "I've come to save the day," Ricky erases it, saying, "They'd understand that he's a superhero already." I'm unsure whether by "They'd understand . . ." Ricky means his writing audience or the starfish under attack, but either way, his awareness of multiple perspectives is growing; he is thinking with sophistication about his writing.

Ricky also pushes back when he senses that I don't understand his audience well enough. After I make one suggestion, Ricky resists adding written text, saying, "I think everyone in this class would know that." And when I point out that he could put a label beside his very first picture of Pufferfish on page two, Ricky asserts, "I just want him to be the only thing in that picture." He explains that he likes the visual effect of this picture when compared to the very last scene on page two, where Pufferfish blows up to enormous size to challenge Archie—for Ricky, a climactic and especially humorous moment.

As we near the end of the conference, the story resolution is incomplete. I ask Ricky if he wants to hear an idea, and he agrees. In the story, near the top of page three, Archie saves himself from Pufferfish's assault of spikes by bending his body out of the way in a virtual, "fourth dimension" way—as characters do in one of Ricky's favorite movies, *The Matrix*. Here, Ricky has written a speech bubble, where Archie proudly declares, "You didn't know I was a black belt in *Matrix* style fighting." This is the point at which the story has stalled. I say to Ricky: "Hey, what if Pufferfish also likes *The Matrix*? What if Archie and Pufferfish actually have something in common?" Ricky looks up and ponders the idea. He seems to like it. He says: "They could become sidekicks together!" A resolution is in sight. I leave Ricky to develop an ending.

Experiencing Writing as Enjoyable and Socially Purposeful

Ricky's writing appropriates and interweaves multiple popular sources—a Hollywood science fiction movie, superhero storylines, humorous allusions such as "the turtle signal!" (à la the "bat signal" in *Batman*), as well as references to a popular book series for kids, Captain Underpants. He's engaged by playful characters and seems especially connected to the "sidekick"— that is, a close companion or underling figure to a hero. Like Martin and Carla, Ricky's most engaged and motivated writing does not come from writing about himself, almost as if such realistic writing fails to capture his actual experience. In putting together "The Adventures of Archie the Turtle," Ricky draws instead upon a blend of images and genres to shape something he can call his own. He enjoys manipulating pieces of popular media and sharing his emerging work with others. Ricky is working on giving voice, in writing, to what he wants to say—and he appears to need space where visual images can drive and sustain his thinking.

Ricky also benefits from opportunities to experience writing, most fundamentally, as enjoyable and socially purposeful—for his writing to have direct relational consequences. "Archie the Turtle" will be successful if it makes Ricky's peers smile and laugh—for example, when the "turtle signal" shines, when Pufferfish blows up to full size, or when Archie dodges danger with his *Matrix*-style move. The reactions of his peers to these moments, and his own enjoyment of these scenes, are the payoff. Ricky also has needed time with partners in workshop, with those who are a bit more confident and fluent in conventional writing, to experience what Lave and Wenger (1991) call "legitimate peripheral participation"—simply observing and being around purposeful activity in a community as a mediating step before taking up the practices of that community. Such social experiences, with Ricky perhaps playing a sidekick role himself, have allowed Ricky a space to participate with others in developing and representing ideas, and to gradually experiment with writing on his own.

In these ways, Ricky benefits from a context in which social connection, flexible expectation, and experimentation with language are possible, where an emphasis on participation outweighs rigidly defined products. In our workshop, as in Martin's, visual images have led the way in Ricky's thinking—creating the means, the footing, by which written words and prose become meaningful and motivating. With support, Ricky takes his own steps to establish a writer's confidence and identity. Indeed, as we conferenced, Ricky articulated a powerful connection between his own writing and the work of "an artist"—that is, one doing something personal and original, who nevertheless must keep an observer's perspective in mind. The connection between author and artist reminds me of Carla's developing writer identity, and how visual imagining, for both Carla and Ricky, has helped produce writing that is both playful and socially purposeful, heightening motivation and allowing students to experience writing as intriguing, worthwhile, and real.

CONCLUDING THOUGHTS

Given substantial choice in a workshop setting, several of our upper elementary writers were driven to engage popular and visual spheres, through which they accessed and created multisensory worlds, generated writing content, experimented with symbolic representation, and built connections with peers. This was perhaps especially true for students who had the least confidence with conventional writing. Shared media—like the Captain Underpants series, *SpongeBob SquarePants*, *The Matrix*, and Chronicles of Narnia, for example—provided not just mutual worlds around which students could communicate but existing genres, forms, and characters that young writers could tap into, experiment with, and modify. In effect, such popular worlds were akin to scaffolds—language structures, character types, and plot devices permeating students' social, cultural, and mental universes from which they could generate language and say something about the world. Our role, as we saw it, was not to ward off such popular connections but to help students access, filter, and represent what was clearly in and on their minds.

Locating Both Confidence and Challenge in Writing

Writer agency and originality, as demonstrated in this chapter, showed itself in the tweaking, rearranging, or retelling of popular media narratives in new ways, as when Ricky used sea creatures and repurposed a scene from *The Matrix* to tell a whimsical hero story. In such self-directed writing initiatives, students became invested in their work, which seemed to flow from the time and space available to locate a personally meaningful, accessible writing zone, one in which they could feel both confidence and challenge. Confidence emerged as they re-created worlds and texts, often visually, with which they were deeply familiar and interested. Personal knowledge and expertise was a driving force for such confidence, like Martin's knowledge of specific video games. Challenge came from representing, tweaking, and modifying familiar worlds—depicting the intricacies of Mario's game world, reimagining a popular children's book for peers, or telling a superhero narrative in a funny way. Even small forms of agency and originality, with otherwise borrowed media, represented significant and useful challenges, and some students would devotedly spend hours on such writing—in some cases, losing themselves in a piece and working through recess time. Such engagement seemed to emerge from self-directed, purposeful writing choices, student-centered expertise, social support, and the opportunity to generate the right amount of challenge for oneself.

Respecting the Power of Visual Imagination

A second realization is the obvious power of the visual dimension. Martin, Carla, and Ricky each integrated visualized worlds in different ways. Martin's drawings allowed him to represent meaningful worlds to himself—and eventually became a way to give others access to his video game interests, which sponsored active oral communication in the classroom. Such drawings provided the groundwork for engaged talk, facilitated primarily by adults, which nurtured shared understandings and experimentation with written codes—all important areas of growth for Martin. Carla, by contrast, seemed to use drawing for immediate social purposes, offering an "Idea Book" to help others write, as if conscious of the challenge of thinking and writing imaginatively in workshop. Aware of her own vulnerability with conventions, of the norms by which her writing attempts might be rejected, she takes up an author-artist stance where her visual talents can thrive, even while serving "official" (Dyson, 2013) school writing goals. Ricky, in some ways similar to Martin, uses drawing to generate a visual world that he finds entertaining and that can sponsor oral communication in terms of his 4th-grade interests. Like Carla and Martin both, Ricky enacts a hybrid writing identity—writer/cartoonist[1]—where visual images drive and sustain meaningful worlds, and eventually language use, making "writing" a sensible, enjoyable, playful act.

For such students, visual domains during workshop went beyond merely illustrating what had already been written as an afterthought to writing. Although some of our students illustrated their works in precisely this way (after the fact), for Martin, Carla, and Ricky drawing had to come first or be intermixed with acts of "writing"—as a resource from which to generate and sustain symbolic thinking and active oral, social communication. Indeed, we might have short-circuited writer growth and engagement by cutting off access to visual imagination, assuming that such drawing was off task or only for primary-age writers (see Sousanis [2015] for an academic dissertation written in the form of a graphic novel). This is a particularly significant point with respect to upper elementary English language learners. Samway (2006) writes that "drawing provides a valuable rehearsal for writing, yet many older ELLs are urged to write without the benefit of this experience" (p. 78). Indeed, our workshop each year included students for whom visual imagination in many ways constituted, or at least richly facilitated, thinking and engagement, assisting and complementing language production significantly and gradually shaping purposeful use of conventional codes.

Expanding Our Notions of Writing Practice

A final implication involves basic assumptions about text, communication, and writing—about what "counts" as literate practice. Our students tended to write less about themselves and were less drawn toward "personal narrative" as commonly taught in schools. Instead, many craved opportunities to process popular media inputs—Hollywood stories, images, and characters, interactive video game worlds, popular books, images and TV series, and the powerful new technologies surrounding them (Dyson, 1997, 2003). Of course, this *was* a way of writing about themselves. Self-driven acts of writing in a public setting provided a forum for students to manage and respond to the powerful role of media sources in their lives, which necessarily involved the visual domain. In this sense, workshop allowed students to grasp and respond to the tools and images of popular culture. Rather than ignoring or positioning popular media as nonacademic and unworthy, flexible norms helped students connect with these as active literacy sources—to make sense, even in small ways, of a changing, media-intensive world.

Such guidance was not without discomfort and tension at times for adults. We had to adjust to story grammars, like Martin's, that we initially did not recognize, and to the tendency of some students to rely on visual representation almost exclusively. We regularly revisited questions of how much drawing, for example, met a writer's needs, as well as our own vision for workshop. When does this type of drawing reflect a productive learning zone and when does it not? To what extent do we insist on certain "kinds" of writing from students, for certain "amounts" of prose or narrative text from students? On the other hand, to what extent had we already limited students too much—by ignoring things like "video" as text (Wohlwend, 2013)? We engaged such questions in situated fashion—that is, less through fixed classroom policy or quantitative prescription and more as each case presented itself, based on the needs of individual students, previous production, and how far along we were in the year.

In general, we sought to create a social, democratic space where relationships mattered and where oral language, drawing, writing, and reading interacted to shape meaningful forms of communication and action. Indeed, we felt that Martin, Carla, and Ricky had found, given the conditions of our workshop, "sweet spots" in writing development, giving us unique and robust insights into their strengths and needs. As potentially marginalized students, they became instead invested writers, showing self-driven independence, creativity, energy, and a desire to communicate socially. They produced and published work in the classroom of which they were rightly proud—even as we all understood that there was more writing development to come.

QUESTIONS FOR REFLECTION

- What do you see as the relationship between drawing, oral language, and writing?
- What role does Martin's knowledge of video games play in forming a foundation for his writing?
- How comfortable would you be allowing a student like Martin to draw video games during writing workshop? What tensions might you experience?
- What do you see as Carla's needs in relation to her identity and confidence as a writer and as a peer?
- What kind of feedback, if any, would you give Carla on her misspellings?
- In what ways does Ricky's comic drawing qualify as valuable writing to you?
- What writing standards are reflected in Ricky's process with "The Adventures of Archie the Turtle?"

CHAPTER 3

Conferencing and Literacy Desiring
Trusting Students as Writers

Conferencing with students during workshop, listening and coaching as 4th-graders produced writing that reflected their own goals, constituted the majority of my time in Mr. Allegro's classroom. Students regularly sought interaction with adults, and conferences usually emerged organically as 4th-graders requested support or as we checked in with individuals and pairs. Getting to all students who wanted a conference was a bit challenging, even with volunteers, and students understood that they could not always access an adult for feedback. Per our blue sheet process, which provided a guide for steps to take in developing a piece of writing (see Chapter 1), students were directed to conduct peer conferences before requesting an adult conference. However, meeting with an adult often seemed to be a preferred mode, and an adult conference "waiting list" became a regular feature on the classroom whiteboard. Students would write their names on the board—first come, first served—if they wanted feedback. Conferences themselves could be as brief as a few seconds, amounting to a quick brainstorm around new writing, an affirmation, or simple suggestion—or they could last 10 minutes or more, especially if we were privileged •enough to have additional volunteers.

No matter the interaction, great discipline was required on the part of adults to listen to what kids were saying and doing. Indeed, in conferencing, I found it easy to crowd out students' concerns with my own, and I observed numerous times when volunteers did the same. Navigating between what I thought should happen in writing and what a student might be thinking was a humbling, powerful daily exercise in our workshop. It required apprenticing to the worldview of a child, decentering my own perceptions. Calkins et al. (2003) assert that a key step in any writing conference is to "weigh whether you want to accept or alter the child's current plans and processes" (p. v). Such "weighing" is precisely what I found complex. There were intricacies in "accepting or altering" a child's plans in a workshop driven by participation, play, and exploration.

Becoming better at listening is a deceptively difficult practice. In listening, we are often guided by our own expectations of acceptable endpoints and outcomes. Our perceptions are mediated by the "official" curriculum, which, as Dyson (2013) suggests, makes it difficult to perceive the intriguing "unofficial" writing practices of students. Olsson (2009), an early childhood educator, points out further that we tend to look for what we already know as we imagine children—for what we expect "should be" there. We use preset goals, personal assumptions, a belief in knowledge as given, or trust in child development itself as an orderly set of stages, to project onto children what they should be doing and learning. When we do not see what we expect, and when student energy and desire go in unexpected directions, we surmise that something is wrong. I myself found it hard to escape the logic of these beliefs as I worked with students, which the vignettes below reveal.

In this chapter, I introduce an unconventional term, *literacy desiring*, which some theorists (Kuby & Gutshall Rucker, 2015, 2016; Leander & Boldt, 2012; Olsson, 2009) have employed recently to expand our usual perceptions of language learning. Literacy desiring emphasizes the holistic, in-the-moment, full-bodied ways in which students are drawn into and energized by a range of textual engagements. The term *desiring* resists more common figures of speech such as literacy *skills*, *abilities*, *products*, and even writing *processes*—that focus on design, tools (for the future), and endpoints. The term *desiring* also challenges our habitual language regarding student "needs"—which are typically understood as deficits.[1] By contrast, Kuby and Gutshall Rucker (2015) write:

> The literacy desiring we conceptualize is about the present processes of producing —a force, a becoming, a coming together of flows and intensities. . . . Our intent with literacy desiring is to focus on the intra-actions of people-with-materials, -movements, and -surprises while creating, not necessarily a future end product. (p. 315)

Here, attention is drawn to "flows and intensities" of literacy engagements, and to the "surprises" that occur as children engage in writing. Teachers and researchers seek to understand the ways that students exhibit energy, emotional resonance, and bodily engagement with and around texts. Leander and Boldt (2012), from this perspective, emphasize the phrase *affective intensities*—moments of heightened connection and engagement, even excitement—as central to literacy practice and research. Such a nonconventional perspective calls us to place greater value on when and how literacy "intensities" and "desiring" emerge, to better understand what such moments consist of and what students are accomplishing through them. (For a related point with respect to reading practices with older children, see Wilhelm and Smith [2014].)

Olsson (2009) argues likewise that teachers and researchers must start "from the idea that things are already going on [with children] and that one's task is to go in and try to latch on to these things" (p. 181).

Teachers must learn to attach to the energy and motivation already present—walking *with* student motivations, seeking to understand the problem already at work—rather than simply replacing it with an adult goal or standard. Such a stance emphasizes that we engage with more than isolated writing skills when we conference, and that such skills are always part of a set of interconnected interests, purposes, actions, and material realities—or what philosophers Deleuze and Guattari (1987) refer to as an "assemblage." Texts become "participants" in the world (Leander & Boldt, 2012); they *do* things—writers "use them, move with and through them, in the production of intensity" (p. 25). This view of texts invites us to recognize the presence of multiple overlapping forces in writing events, as literacy desiring is pursued. In conferencing, we should prepare ourselves for the fact that we may not know everything about writing—that we have things to learn—and that surprises will occur.

Below, I present two conferences with students, from different years, arguing that conferencing interactions were crucial opportunities for students to make unique writing practices visible, and for adults not simply to "help" but to work on listening and "latching on" to the complex motivations and desires of students.

LEARNING TO LATCH ON TO STUDENTS' GOALS

February 12, Year 2: 9:30 A.M. As I arrive today, the kids are well into a Valentine's project. Mr. Allegro is modeling for students how to glue two pieces of black construction paper cut out in the shape of hearts. He has kids glue these two pieces with colored tissue paper between them. He says, "Remember: Don't glob, just glue," then shows students how to trim the edges of the tissue paper. He alludes to the fact that workshop is coming up soon and says the next step in the Valentine's project will happen later this afternoon.

Students gradually transition to writers' workshop. There is no minilesson today. A few students get classroom laptops from the cart; a few partner teams go outside; pairs form, talking about ideas. I overhear Terence and Steven talking animatedly: "We're going to work on 'Super-Leprechaun' for St. Patrick's Day . . . and read it *on* St. Patrick's Day!" Another student who is listening chimes in: "I love St. Patrick's Day." A holiday focus has permeated writing this year, something that didn't happen last year. There are three volunteer parents today—me and two moms, one holding an infant. One volunteer asks if I can help her son, Cameron, bind (publish) his story. He is proud of his accomplishment, "Laser World." It's about seven pages, neatly typed and well edited. His mom is right there and celebrates with him as I finish the binding process. She's had a positive hand in this, especially with the typing.

9:53 A.M.: I pause and take note of what the kids are doing. It's hard to capture the multiple worlds at work, and I know I'm missing a great deal. Terence is reading a story idea back to Steven. They have filled in a planning page, and Terence reads a summary of what the plot will be. I guess that Terence is doing most of the actual writing, but Steven—who seems to talk a great deal but write little—is clearly offering a lot. They seem content, even excited, to be working together. I overhear, "We can have guest appearances by Super Santa!"

Cameron is already back to work. He and a partner are making a title page for a new story, called "The Valentine Boys and the Big Bad Heartbreak." Several students are involved in drawing. Vicky is looking through a cartoon-technique book and is drawing a few figures rather than writing. My guess is that she's working something out for a story—I will need to check with her. Mandy is drawing an image with her colored pencils. Calvin asks me about a picture he's drawn: He asks if it looks like a pot, and I say yes. I learn later that this is part of a story he's working on about zombies, but Cameron's mom, a consistent volunteer, points out that he's been drawing for the past 2 weeks and hasn't written anything without an adult pushing for this or writing with him. She's concerned.

I overhear Steven saying to Terence, "Once we write the story, we'll see what happens after that."

Mr. Allegro is working intently with Kent, reviewing what's written on a laptop screen in front of them. Michelle is still putting together her Valentine project. Ronny is typing intently on a laptop. Isabel is working across from him, rereading her work. Next to me, Damien is writing a story and reads part of it to Vicky, who's sitting across from him. They are playing with words. I overhear him saying the word *flashback* and Vicky giving him ideas. She says, "It could be 'Flashback, applejack'. . . ." In Damien's story, titled "Cat Got Your Tongue?," the narrator writes the word *Flashback* as a subtitle, as if to lead into a flashback memory, but then a cat named Jack interrupts the narrator, because he thinks he's being spoken to. "Flashjack?" the cat interjects.

How Much to Revise on Valentine's Day

10:05: Isabel and Angel ask for a conference. We run through the blue sheet process, and they report that in a peer conference Vicky liked the story and gave them just a few surface corrections to make. I suspect that the peer conference has been cursory, but rather than send them back, I invite them to read to me. Angel and Isabel take turns reading their story aloud. It's about a girl who writes a special Valentine to her "secret crush," but the message gets lost in translation. The boy who was supposed to get the Valentine assumes it came from a different girl—from the most popular girl in the school, someone they have fictionally named Kate Henderson. The narrator is upset; this was not her plan. However, in the end things work out. The secret crush eventually comes by the narrator's house and gives her a Valentine. The twists and misunderstandings in the story are what make it work, along with themes of mistaken identity and hidden desire. The girls mark it a 5 on the blue sheet, the highest score they can give (see Chapter 1 for a description of the rating system).

I struggle with what kind of feedback to give them. I certainly like the story, but I want to push them a bit. We've told students that a 5 means they should expect feedback and be prepared to revise and improve their work. For example, in this story, they seem to rush to the resolution too quickly. There is room to enrich the scenes, to build up the overall tension, to add descriptive detail. The problem, however, is that revision takes time. Angel and Isabel want this piece to function *today*, not next week, when Valentine's Day is past. They are not especially interested in revising, which might technically "improve" the story but only in an abstract, adult-oriented sense. Such "improvement" is seemingly distant from their own sense of quality, which is connected to *timeliness*, to the energy of today.

We reread page one aloud, and I decide to ask them questions that come to me, initially focused on detail: "So why didn't the narrator write her name on the Valentine?" (The obvious answer—it was a "secret crush.") "How old is your narrator?" I discover that she's in 4th grade, but Isabel argues that no detail here is needed. She says that readers will be able to *tell* this is 4th grade, because, as she says, "2nd-graders wouldn't think this way, and 6th-graders probably don't do Valentines." The girls express a great deal of social awareness, and I suspect they have another reason for not disclosing the grade level—perhaps not wanting to spawn audience suspicion that the story reflects their own affectionate interests. I ask if they want to give the "secret crush" a name, but they say it's better to be mysterious. I'm struggling to pose useful questions, although there is certainly room for writing growth, for better crafting of this piece.

Yet, too much emphasis on "revision" itself seems to be part of the problem. Revising eclipses *their* goal. This isn't just about writing skills; it's about an event, *today*, Valentine's Day (which occurs on Saturday this year), and beyond that, it's about emerging and compelling social realities in their lives: sexuality, gender, attraction, relationships—new territory. They're giddy about this piece. And they've put good work into it. The time to strike is now. Angel and Isabel want my approval, but even more than that, they want me, in Olsson's (2009) words, to "latch on" to their excitement and energy (p. 181).

I'm not so great at this in the moment. But we do reach a compromise. We finally agree that they can work on revising a bit next week—that we won't bind or publish now—but that it's definitely good enough to read aloud today during sharing time. This works for them. Sharing time is powerful. I write down that their goal for next week, before publishing, will be to focus on adding details—one or two significant additions, something to enhance the plot and vividly strike their readers. Next week, we'll look at some "vivid phrases" we've been posting on the board as models. Yet, even as I write this, I'm aware that the "secret crush" story is *already* vivid to them. Indeed, the story would make an amazing and timely text for a 4th-grade discussion, raising questions about "liking" people, mistaken identity, gender, status, name-calling. It's rich territory for second-semester 4th grade.

Helping Students Continue in a Flow

My goal here is less to explain "how to" conduct a conference and more to revisit assumptions about what students need from us in writing interactions. What kind of expertise is most valuable? For me, I tend to forward my own writing knowledge and instincts, trying to get kids to reflect on writing by posing questions and seeing their writing from an outsider's or reader's perspective. I try to make my own "cognition" visible, hoping that students will glean strategies from my modeling, that they will adopt similar questioning practices themselves. This approach aims less toward perfect or accurate "form" in writing and more toward strategic thinking on students' part, which can lead to more in-depth writing.

The tension I experience above is whether Angel and Isabel should, in fact, work to "improve" their piece of writing on these terms, or whether I need to "latch on" to *their* purpose and energy. I struggle with this. How easy it is to take the wind out of a writer's sails! Or simply to miss the wider range of what their writing might mean to them. This doesn't imply that I should never draw on my expertise or that we should never revise. But it does suggest a different kind of awareness on my part, the need for new considerations. Perhaps my hallowed questioning practices are limiting, even demotivating to students—tone-deaf to the moment, to the literacy desiring that is at work—making these 4th-graders wonder how and when writing is *ever* valuable, and for whom.

A stance that respects literacy desiring shifts our gaze from predetermined expertise. As Dahlberg and Moss (2009) suggest, the focus is, rather, "to follow how the learning processes proceed and their power to continue" (p. xxii). This stance emphasizes "following" learning in the moment, observing how energy is "continuing." Beyond asking ourselves "How can writers improve their coherence, detail, or point?" we must also ask: "What helps them continue in a flow?" This seems especially important given the common exhaustion that writers can feel through their writing efforts. Meier (2011) explains that children often resist editing and revising because they "are physically tired and lack the energy to go back and revise" (p. 100). Workshop, in this respect, has not magically motivated students to want to revise their papers, but instead it helps make visible the multiple components that feed Angel and Isabel's energy—the dynamics and presence of a holiday; emerging awareness of sexuality, gender, and attraction; their own friendship and partnership, the fact that they are exploring this territory *together*; narrative as a tool; and a larger classroom context and audience that might be interested, to whom they hope to display their newly charted reality. The "text" here is *one* item among many pieces in an "assemblage," and our preoccupation with just one piece, the abstract "quality" of the text, might miss the larger event that is going on.

Workshop provides a way for me to navigate this dilemma—specifically through our sharing forum. Public sharing offers new layers for what "being done" with writing might mean. Reading the Valentine's piece aloud to classmates fulfills a key purpose for Angel and Isabel—one that likely outshines the written revisions they will make next week. Indeed, Angel and Isabel took turns reading their story aloud at the end of class, and even though a few students didn't listen well (a conflict between two peers emerged and became distracting, with one student staring in anger at the other), and although Mr. Allegro had to refocus the class and ask Isabel and Angel to read more loudly, by the end, students (at least those near the front of class) were highly engaged in the plot. There was good applause as they finished, although, sadly, no time was left for questions. Sharing writing in this way became another way of "revising" and "completing" the text—of having it fulfill an active function—and perhaps even of assessing whether enough detail existed.

For Angel and Isabel, growth and energy around revising may come when they sense first that someone can enter into their space with them—that an adult, in this case, "gets" or is willing to seek what they are after. In retrospect, simple mirroring affirmations, such as "Wow, the narrator seems to like him a lot" or "She's in a complicated situation, isn't she?" might have been more useful. Rather than posing questions (my usual approach), mirroring the emotional resonance of a piece can help writers feel heard, allowing for further talk, connection, and elaboration on students' terms. In this particular case, I suspect that a direct affirmation might also have been called for: "You *have* to share this today!"

Beyond affirmation, constructive feedback might best be situated—not based in general processes of what "all" 4th-graders need but connected to particular students and a particular moment. Rather than my usual concerns about descriptive detail, what questions might enter into the flow of the "problem" students are working on in this story and on this day in particular? For example, if Angel and Isabel eagerly wish to present this piece *today*, given the singular energy of the Valentine's holiday, how might my feedback work with this goal more directly? For example, what do they most need for the presentation to come off as they hope? What goals do they have for sharing time? To what extent might I need to let go of the need to "revise" this time, at least as I conceive of it? Writing growth, and a desire to revise, I suggest here, may evolve as children come to direct their own intensities, shaping and experiencing, in the moment and on the right timeline, the value of their own literacy desiring in the classroom.

RESPONDING TO CONFUSING WRITING: MACIE'S STORY

Next, I track my work with one writer over several sessions during our fourth year of the workshop. Macie's writing followed a narrative mode that I didn't easily recognize. Trying to understand her work and "improve" her narrative skills brought me to wrestle with my own assumptions and starting points. Macie shares an evolving story that moves in eclectic directions and that she herself struggles to summarize. I listen sympathetically, but find it hard to know what steps to take and how her self-driven writing instincts can be both celebrated and nurtured in the direction of what I consider to be writing growth. I confront questions such as: What limits exist in following or building upon a student's own literacy desiring? What does "growth" mean for students whose skills seem especially weak but who are also learning what it is they want to say, and do, in a writing classroom? How does a focus away from endpoints, more grounded in participation and writing as exploration, serve a student like Macie? A challenging degree of listening was called for in this case, raising questions in me about what I was listening *for* and what was being enabled or hindered in the process.

Olsson (2009) encourages a broad view of children's sense-making, pointing out that incoherence and even "nonsense" are often "the very means by which we make sense" (p. 113). Young children, for example:

> play with language through inventing it again. . . . They invent new languages never before heard of. . . . This is often the approach that children have not only toward language but towards most things they learn; everything is potentially otherwise and not static. (p. 114)

This stance looks for "the production of sense" in a wide field, one that includes what we sometimes may think of as incoherence. Such a commitment, Olsson (2009) says, shifts everything for the child, who is no longer seen as someone "who always has everything wrong" (p. 182). Conceiving sense and nonsense, coherence and incoherence, as interconnected (rather than as mutually excluding) "makes it possible to re-evaluate young children's sayings and doings, to take them seriously and to see them as contributions to the world, to see them as added constructions of the world" (p. 182). Such a stance does not mean that adults and children engage in meaningless communication. What matters is that we are open to meanings that we may not initially follow—and to writing as an assemblage of actions not confined to the text itself. We must be careful not to dismiss things that do not immediately fit into preconceived categories. This has implications, especially for the language expressions of nonmajority writers, new language learners, and alternatively developing writers, whose attempts may be less recognizable or less clearly coherent to adults.

Resisting a Ranking Stance

January 12, Year 4: Macie comes over to me silently as if she wants me to see her work, but she doesn't say anything. She's holding some writing, so I inquire. Her story is about a mommy cat and a baby cat. The top half of the page has scrawled handwriting and the bottom half has a drawing of two cats. I invite Macie to sit with me and to read the top half. "Mommy I'm so hungry! . . ." she reads from the page. The baby cat's voice is what we hear for a few sentences. There is minimal punctuation and no other voice. Page two then goes on to adopt a different narrative voice—one more distant, informative, outside the story, telling us "about" cats.

I want to support Macie in building her writing from the initial scene she's set, especially around the baby's hunger. I first ask if she wants me to ask some questions about the story. I am learning the importance of asking this simple question in workshop conferences—that is, checking in first to see if questions, in fact, are desired. Sometimes, other responses are more helpful: listening, mirroring back, rereading, reenacting, drawing, smiling, relating to the story ("Oh, that reminds me of . . ."), or affirmation. Sometimes it is the student who has the question or comment to make. Although I always have several questions to ask while reading a writer's work, young writers do not always enter conferences assuming that adult questions should be at the center. I've also noticed ways in which this assumption, on my part, has broken the flow of energy. I try to ask now: "What kinds of things are you working on?" or "Tell me about . . ." or "Are you interested in hearing some of my questions or thoughts?" Starting in this way seems to give writers respect as well as agency in how we might learn together and what they might learn from me. Indeed, to respond "yes," to ask for questions or feedback, is risky, opening young writers up to critical attention—something not every student (or even adult) writer is ready for immediately after composing.

Macie says she is open to questions, so I focus on the opening scene: "Why was this kitty so hungry?" I ask. Macie answers, and I record some of her response: "Mom tried to get her food but she couldn't because she had another baby in her stomach. So the baby kitty ran around trying to get food." I ask other questions, trying to get a feel for this story-world: "What did her mother do in response?" "Are the kitties wild, or do they have human owners who feed them?" After a brief conversation, Macie stops to write the following on her paper: "tring [trying] to get food."

Earlier that same day, I had worked with two highly fluent and confident writers. Amanda, for example, keeps a "Writers' Workshop Folder," which has an opening page with a "to-do list," under which she has checked off eight out of 10 items. Today, she showed me three pages of a delightfully written, single-spaced draft, "Mr. Penguin's Trip to Egypt." This is a new installment of a series she started last year on her own. Last year, Amanda tells me, she wrote "Mr. Penguin's Trip to France." Earlier today, I also worked with Rebecca, an unusually strong writer, whose early drafting offers rich detail and complex, interweaving plots around fantasy-oriented themes. The workshop gives Rebecca the space she needs to soar, and adults often stand back and simply encourage her exploration, with comments to other adults like "Wow."

As this day ends, I find myself reflecting on the difference between working with precocious students like Amanda and Rebecca and working with Macie. The stance I am working on is a respect for, and embrace of, each individual learner's space, rather than another stance that competes in my mind—namely, surprise at, or emphasis on, "ability differences," a kind of comparing or ranking stance. This is not an easy shift, but I'm trying to preoccupy myself less with ranking students along a single, assumed line of competence.

Macie Finds Her Own Way

January 26: Macie and I meet to talk about her writing. She is sitting at a small table that Mr. Allegro has cleaned off for the day. Macie reads me her work—the same kitty story—and there are now three chapters, plus chapter "½." The story has changed somewhat from the first version. On each page, something almost completely different happens. Page one is the kitty, now designated as a baby tiger, crying for food. Page two is the kitty being tired and wanting to go home and see her friend "Ticke." On page three, a comet hits the ground and the kitty gets burned. Then she sees a polar bear that tells her to go through a cave to save her mom.

The pieces are loosely related, but much of this appears to reflect a kind of "What next?" strategy—something that I learned in graduate school to be a common pitfall with narrative writing. In the "What next?" strategy, a writer generates an event but then simply keeps asking "What next?" to produce more writing, rather than aiming for a central impact, idea, or impression. Stories move forward from event to event, with little internal coherence and a less compelling effect on readers. We tend to be bored by such stories, or ask "So what?" Macie's progression here seems particularly problematic; the connections between scenes are hard for me to fathom. Macie rarely brings earlier material into new scenes—except in chapter "½." Here, Macie *has* followed up on what happened in Chapter 1, based on the questions I asked in our first conference. She has answered my queries—saying, for example, why the kitty was hungry, who each voice represents (Molly is the baby kitty and Allie is the mom), and how the kitty usually gets fed. Chapter "½" is telling, however. The title fraction suggests that responding to my questions has been an aside from Macie's main thinking. It's not quite worthy of being a real chapter.

Unsure how to proceed, I tell Macie, "Well, one thing I see in your chapters is that they are surprising—I don't know what's going to happen next." Macie smiles at this. I mention that in my own writing, one way I come up with ideas is to look back to what's happened before, and then bring something from the previous writing into the new section. I want her to consider ways of linking things together. I give an example, showing how Ticke (from Chapter 2) might reappear in the story. But Macie isn't thrilled by this concept. She has her mind on a new scene—yet another "What next?" If anything, Macie values being able to do this on her own, making her own decisions and taking the story, such as it is, where she wants.

February 2: Macie comes over and sits at the table next to me. She makes herself present for adult support, but does not directly ask for conferencing time. She has an illustrated reference book on animal life with her. When I eventually ask what she's looking up, she says, "I'm trying to find animals for my story." She wants Molly and Allie to meet some other creatures. She also says that the kitties will be poisoned. As she pages through the book, she comes upon a sizeable picture of a tarantula and says, "Ooh, look at that spider." The spider is large and gruesome, and I make a face. I then say, "Oh, what if the animal they meet is a spider!"

Macie says, "No, I don't like tarantulas."

I venture, "Well, what if the poison came from the tarantula?" I realize that tarantulas may not, in fact, be poisonous, but before I can retract the statement, Macie says, "Good idea."

I feel somewhat outside of Macie's writing process. It pursues its own logic, a logic I don't easily follow and to which I only incidentally make contributions. At the table, Macie turns a few times to plastic sea life figures on the nearby shelf and touches them. She picks up and shows me two figures of baby turtles coming out of their eggs. She then gets up and decides to show a peer the spider picture. "I'm gonna show Russell," she says. "Where is he?" Russell is away from the computer, over by his desk. Macie walks across the room, where she and Russell have an exchange. All I hear as she walks back is Russell saying, "You don't want them to die!" Apparently, Russell is concerned about the cats being poisoned, as if Macie is pondering a grave narrative mistake—killing off her main characters. Macie soon has the reference book open and is now showing the tarantula picture to anyone who might be interested. Not many are looking up, but Macie is walking silently through the classroom, displaying the picture.

Back at her desk, Macie says that Allie and Molly are going to meet a sea turtle and then get poisoned by a spider.

February 16: Macie is stapling together her five-chapter story of Molly and Allie, which she has finished over the past 2 weeks. She says Mr. Allegro has asked her to write a summary of the story. "I don't know how to do a summary," she tells me. We sit down to conference, and I learn that she is very ready to move on to a new piece of writing, but she is open to this last step, especially if she can type it on a laptop. Rather than leaving her to do the typing, I read the story aloud to her, and we work on summarizing things orally. I ask: "So what's this story about?"

Macie responds, "It's about cats who go on adventures." She goes on: "Molly meets a polar bear. She gets pulled into the ocean by a crab. . . ." She runs through the events of each chapter. I selectively record what she says. As I write, I let Macie know that summaries leave some things out in order to relay only the most important points. I reiterate these things aloud as I write. I remind her to think about what happens in the beginning. She looks back and says, "Oh, the kittens are very hungry." By the end, my written summary goes like this:

> It's about cats who go on adventures. In the beginning, Molly becomes very hungry. Molly meets a polar bear, gets pulled into the ocean, and she meets a mermaid. Her mom dies and she has to take care of her 4-year-old sister and two twins.

The last sentence reflects Chapters 4 and 5, which Macie has worked on recently. I've provided significant support for the summary, especially by recording only the main events and by reorganizing the order. For example, Macie had stated, "Her mom dies" last when summarizing verbally, but as she spoke I suggested that we place this episode earlier to reflect the story order. I also suggested the language, "In the beginning . . ."

To gain clarification myself, I make a little character map of what I think is happening at the end. Showing Macie the diagram, I say, "Allie is the mom. She had Molly and a younger baby, who is now 4 years old. But Molly is now a teenager and has twins herself. Right?" I continue: "Allie dies, and now Molly has to take care of her little sister *and* her own twins." I draw a circle around the 4-year-old and the twins to show who Molly has to take care of.

Macie says, "Yeah, that's right."

I say, "Wow, that's a lot of responsibility for Molly."

Macie nods seriously, and says, "Yes." Then she adds, "And she's only 16."

I invite Macie to type the summary herself now, suggesting that she can build from what I've already written. After a few moments, she types in her first sentence: "Allie dies." She says aloud, "I thought I might mix it up a little." After a pause, she elaborates: "I want the reader to know what happens to Allie, so they don't have to wait." I remind her that a summary identifies a "big picture" in its first sentence. I point out that readers will not know if Allie is a person, friend, or cat—or if this story is about war, a family, or something else. I say that summaries also help readers know the story order, so it might be best to leave Allie's death until later.

Macie listens but does not seem particularly impressed. She keeps typing. Returning several minutes later, I notice that she has rewritten the summary substantially, taking some of my input to heart as well as moving in her own direction:

> A sumery of my story. There are cats who go on advenchers to save Allie. Molly meats a pollerbear who needs her to save Allie or she'll die. And the babby will never know her mother!

How *Is* Macie Learning?

What does it mean to work with a writer like Macie—especially if we draw upon notions such as staying "in the moment" and respecting the "flows and intensities" of literacy desiring (Kuby & Gutshall-Rucker, 2015)? I certainly wrestled with other impulses during conferences—for example, categorizing Macie simply as a student who is academically "low" or with serious learning "needs." At times, I wanted to teach her directly "how to" narrate more effectively, in effect erasing or substantially redirecting her own seemingly wandering story instincts. Latching on to Macie's writing process was counterintuitive to me. Was my listening stance sending the wrong message? Would Macie simply be left with inadequate skills, making her unprepared for future writing tasks, frustrating her future teachers?

Part of what I hope to do in this chapter is to read against such first-line, ingrained responses. I try to reread events from a new point of view. Lenz Taguchi (2010) talks about such perspective-taking as "re-installing" ourselves in learning events, which is not about "becoming the child" but is primarily a process of transforming ourselves:

> contrary to taking a position of someone else, or trying to become the other, this is about re-installing yourself in the event to become different *in yourself*; that is, to put yourself in a process of *change and transformation* to be able to experience the event differently. (p. 172, italics in original)

Such reinstalling does not mean that I fully understand or have figured out precisely what Macie meant in her story. Instead, the process is more about my own learning, pushing back from familiar routines, categorizations of children, and expectations. Lenz Taguchi (2010) writes that the philosopher Deleuze understood ethics itself to be "about a love for what is" rather than what "should be" (p. 176). "What we are interested in," she writes, "is what an organism, a child, a teacher . . . a learning event can *become* in its intra-activity with the surrounding world" (p. 176). I am trying this stance on with Macie—and for myself.

How might I perceive more possibility in Macie's writing, and in this learning event, than I was initially able to see? Macie's process has a unique, unpredictable coherence to it, generated by her own energy and experimentation. Coherence and incoherence appear to operate together. This is not a story that she has mapped out ahead of time, for example. It morphs and moves. She creates and experiments, allowing things to emerge and bubble up. When I say that her writing is "surprising," she smiles. She likes to "mix it up a little." Indeed, Macie's process contrasts substantially with Amanda's, whose Mr. Penguin travel stories follow an established, reliable pattern. Macie's story has a less linear narrative structure, which some scholars connect with non-Western modes of storytelling (Gallas, 1992; Mikkelsen, 1990). Macie "intra-acts" with her environment (Kuby & Gutshall Rucker, 2016; Lenz Taguchi, 2010), engaging physically with material realities—picture books, classmates, and physical figures like the baby turtles. Searching for an animal for her story yielded the picture of a tarantula, which led her to a peer and then to a new initiative: walking around the classroom to display a gruesome picture to classmates—a picture of something she fears. The laptop itself energizes Macie, where her goal revolves at least as much around trying out technology and the act of keyboarding as it does around writing a summary. Macie follows her literacy desiring in an assemblage of actions. Writing, revising, and sense-making emerge along the way—following a coherence and sense that *she* makes, though almost certainly not in sufficiently acceptable form by official standards.

This perhaps is the central issue: whether we choose to measure Macie's work solely by "official" standards. Olsson (2009) reminds us that children "sometimes engage in a production of sense that leads to truths that we as adults can have a very hard time understanding" (p. 116). If so, what forms of coherence and learning recede from vision?

Macie's story, for instance, reveals a dynamic between childhood need, threat, safety, and adult responsibility. Molly the kitty is on a defining journey from infancy and vulnerability toward adulthood, undergoing a reversal and transformation, where Molly must ultimately take over for her mom. (I only learned later, a few years after the events described here, that Macie is an adopted child.) The story does not focus on "small moments" or a "slice of life," which reflect my own biases in narrative writing (I often encourage students to "zoom in" and "focus" on a single event and expand its details). Macie's scope is bigger than I'd imagined. She traces a major life sequence, advancing things on a grander, epic scale. The story tracks birth, sustenance, mothering, adventure, reproduction, and death.

Yet, it would be unfair and mistaken to fix any single meaning here. This wouldn't be true to Macie's own process, in which meanings emerge and transform. As she types her final summary, she shifts things—from the loss of Allie ("Allie dies") to emphasizing the need to "save Allie" while highlighting the future stakes ("And the babby will never know her mother!"). It's not completely clear to me, from the story, which baby is referred to here. Is this the 4-year-old, Molly's "little sister"? Does it refer to 16-year-old Molly's twins? I'm not sure, but the intensity of the realization in Macie's summary is unmistakable.

Workshop made a space for intensity, for Macie to pursue her own literacy desiring, which seemed to include touching base with elemental fears as well as forms of strength (surviving threats, saving her mom, being able to care for others). Indeed, throughout the sequence above, Macie was neither bored nor unmotivated. She was self-directed, intent, figuring something out. Her experimenting spirit was not closed off to outside input. She made herself available for adult support, quietly and graciously. She reached out. She listened. She also consistently showed agency. For example, when my suggestions and questions aimed for a certain kind of internal story coherence, Macie persisted on her own path, separating things that I would put together, starting narrative lines I did not easily track. To her credit, she did not simply adopt adult suggestions. She wanted to tell this story herself, perhaps wanting to know what such agency feels like in writing. Macie's coherence is, thus, less about what her story "means"—how the internal parts line up or how technically sound it is. Instead, it is more about what a young writer is "doing" and how she is "becoming" in a complex environment (Kuby & Gutshall Rucker, 2016; Lenz Taguchi, 2010; Olsson, 2009). She manipulates tools; she engages and manages the responses of others; she tries out language and story forms. Asking "What next?" is an act of creation for Macie, rather than a deficit strategy. She seems to say: What can I create next that is uniquely mine? Macie is trying on being a creator—she is becoming a creator.

For my own part, I am pondering a different shift, from constructing Macie's literacy and writing, and perhaps her very self, as failing to meet an expectation. I am asking: What might Macie need from adults as she develops a writing identity? How *is* she learning? After a few years of our workshop, I'm inclined more to listen and follow than to insist that Macie adopt my own notion of an effective plot. This is not without tension—and it does not mean that I never offer suggestions, critique, or feedback, or that there are not forms of writing in society that Macie will need to learn. But a key "becoming" for me is less in teaching Macie "how to" tell a story and more a matter of listening and engaging with what she is already doing. In this way, a writer like Macie is affirmed, rather than closed down, at her very point of risk-taking and emergence. Her energy continues, and I remain open, available, and able to engage with the new and unexpected.

RESPECTING THE PRESENT MOMENT

Conferencing with students is an ongoing and essential point of contact in any writing workshop. It allows us to get close to student writing; we seek to understand writer strengths and areas of growth. We provide tailored support. We also have a great deal of power. Our assumptions and expectations position students and shape their writing identities. In this chapter, I step back from simply assuming the positive benefit of my own expertise—that students should automatically implement my strategies and recommendations. Instead, I acknowledge that listening is deceptively difficult and try to expand my awareness of things that "are already going on" with students. I try to "latch on" and stay with a flow—that is, to accept and engage difference, those things I do not expect, appreciate, or even fully understand. I ponder places where my own instincts may have missed a larger picture.

Student writing in the scenes above, I assert, moves beyond textual "meaning" itself and is tied to larger events, relationships, and purposes— for example, to a Valentine's Day dynamic that expands beyond the technical features of Angel and Isabel's story—and to a process of participation, creation, and experimentation that itself may be more important for Macie than the actual writing outcome. My conferencing lens embraces literacy desiring, trusting and making room for students' "assembled" writing motivations and their energies in the moment. My aim is not to dismiss standards or conventional writing forms, which have their role to play. My concern is around a loss of perspective, an overfocus on where students "should be" rather than where they are.

Lenz Taguchi (2010) speaks of an "ethics of immanence" as having important consequences for children. The term *immanence* assumes the value of the here and now, the present moment, rather than looking to the expected future or standing outside or above. As an ethical stance, this affects our sense of whether children themselves are worthy of their own imagined worlds and learning processes—those they actually bring to and enact in school. An ethics of immanence, in Olsson's (2009) words:

> includes looking at the world and human beings without letting perception and affection constantly turn towards the negative by focusing on lack or need. . . . Rather, this style will enable us to ask the question of how desire deploys its forces in the everyday life of the [school] as well as within the academic system. (p. 125)

Such a stance shifts from a framework that tends mostly to stand in judgment—that *produces* deficit, almost exclusively for some children—to one that might also affirm emergent learning. This is partly what is at stake. Will Macie always lose in our constructed game of learning? Will Angel and

Isabel be asked to forfeit what is energizing about their Valentine's story? Rather than constantly turning "to the negative," an ethics of immanence gives students a chance to show us who they are as writers, where their motivations lie, and possible pathways to learning.

QUESTIONS FOR REFLECTION

- In what ways do you notice "literacy desiring" among your own students or among children, either within or beyond the classroom?
- What stance toward revision might best help Angel and Isabel grow as writers, in light of the energy they have in regard to their Valentine's story?
- What is the most important dimension, in your view, in terms of "listening" to Macie's process in writing?
- In what ways would stronger direction from adults help or hinder Macie's learning and development as a writer?
- In what ways might you look beyond the "text" itself in considering your students as writers?

CHAPTER 4

How Relationships Influence Writing and Writing Influences Relationships

In the previous chapters, I've alluded to the ways in which social relationships and social action were integrated with writing processes in workshop. In Chapter 2, Carla's drawings are bound up with social goals, with her desire to make friends and to be useful to her classmates. Ricky's cartoon-like piece, "Archie the Turtle," in effect is a form of play with his peers. In Chapter 3, Angel and Isabel's Valentine's story about a "secret crush" is intensely social work, as they work together to make newfound realities about "liking" others visible to peers.

Given flexible parameters, including opportunities for choice and movement, social purposes—such as building relationships, negotiating social hierarchies, and developing identity in community—were consistently visible practices as students planned, shared, and otherwise engaged in writing. Writing was not merely about written processes or products; rather, students used the workshop to *do things* relationally with writing and through writing. They drew upon, and were confronted by, social resources in ways that gave purpose, and sometimes tension, to their acts of communication. They used writing to gesture socially to classmates and adults, or to assert lines of exclusion and inclusion, wrestling along the way with new forms of agency and voice. The workshop helped make visible the various ways that upper elementary learners live and grow within complex communities, as well as ways in which writing can mediate the social tasks of community life.

Below, I illustrate varying ways in which writing experiences became infused with social energy, and how workshop made visible, in the words of Dyson (2010), "not the composing of individual selves, but the complex participatory dynamics by which writing becomes relevant" to children (p. 7). I emphasize how writing and interactions with others occurred together—as "entangled" dimensions through which students developed both as writers and as community members. I borrow the term *entanglement* to emphasize the ways in which such dimensions "cannot be described separately" (Kuby & Gutshall-Rucker, 2016, p. 44), but rather mutually constitute one another. I suggest further the ways in which energy and motivation in writing often were connected with relational work, via the "affective intensities" (Leander & Boldt, 2012; see also Chapter 3) or intensified energy and emotion that arose through various social encounters, exchanges, movements, and negotiations in workshop. Although I see writing as fundamentally relational in nature, writing in flexibly structured environments, I suggest here, supports relational work at an especially important time for upper elementary learners, as they look forward to the heightened social complexity of middle school life.

The workshop scenes below reveal different ways in which social worlds were interrelated with students' writing development. This is relevant to classroom teachers in a few ways. Attention to social worlds expands our notion of what writing is, how it may serve the child, and the uses to which writing is put. More than a skill set or a series of products, writing is a way of participating, of being and becoming someone, in communally defined spaces. To conceive of writing too narrowly—for example, as a technical skill grounded in individual action—limits our understanding of the ways in which elementary students may experience and use literacy for purposeful action in their lives. A relational perspective thus expands the picture of what writers might reveal to us about their learning needs and can help adults observe and identify opportunities for social–emotional growth, as such opportunities interact with writing development. Workshop helped us perceive the way that relationships functioned in the context of literacy development, and usefully guided us in relation to a social curriculum.

I focus on two broad themes below. The first theme is illustrated by students who actively sought connections with others through writing. In these cases, reaching out to partners or working together was never just about the "writing" per se, but instead always incorporated multiple purposes such as affiliation, inclusion, identity, and safety, and involved human dimensions like courage, risk-taking, and power. The second theme involves ways in which students negotiated voice, control, and status as they worked in collaboration with partners. Teachers, I suspect, are highly familiar with such relational dynamics and realities, although these things are seldom understood as part of the literacy curriculum. In each section that follows, I offer first a brief vignette that highlights the section theme and then provide, and comment upon, a more extended narrative.

BUILDING SOCIAL CONNECTIONS THROUGH WRITING

A Shy Student Reaches Out

January 5, Year 4: It is early in the workshop year, and Rebecca has done some active writing outside of class. Her mom is a classroom volunteer and seems to encourage writing at home. Soon after workshop begins today, I overhear Mr. Allegro talking to Rebecca about trying a peer conference. She is ready for this next step in the process but isn't sure which of her fellow students to ask. She seems proud of her work. I overhear Mr. Allegro ask Rebecca to look around the room and think about someone she might conference with. Rebecca responds with reservation: "But I'm shy."

"Is there anyone you don't usually feel so shy with?" Mr. Allegro asks. Rebecca looks around and shakes her head.

A moment later she says, "Oh! Grace. She used to be my partner!" Rebecca heads over to Grace, who is actively writing at a desk, concentrating, in flow with her work. Mr. Allegro watches and, anticipating a possible rejection, he interjects quickly: "Grace is pretty busy now, Rebecca; you might want to—" He stops himself and then says, "Well, what do you say if someone's busy?"

Rebecca pauses, then says, looking at Mr. Allegro, "Do you have a moment?"

Mr. Allegro says, "Yes."

Mr. Allegro's skill stands out in moments like this, suffused as it is with middle-class norms of polite communication. He knows that "breaking in" is an authentic challenge for Rebecca, who is not confident socially. He also knows to keep things in her court—and how to do so gently. Even with a great deal of experience, Mr. Allegro must check his own desire to prescribe the moment. He helps Grace determine for herself how to break in.

Rebecca is soon at Grace's desk, and she reenacts the scene, holding her story in front of her with two hands: "Um, do you have a moment?"

Grace looks up, orients herself, and then says: "Sure!"

Mr. Allegro and I, relieved, look at each other and nod.

Commentary: A charming moment. What of significance has happened? Rebecca uses writing itself and the workshop context to reach out, test, and build a connection. Rebecca's pride in her writing coincides with our classroom expectation to solicit feedback. Yet, initiating a conversation around writing, on her own, is difficult. She identifies herself as "shy." Breaking into the flow of others involves risk—possibly irritating someone, experiencing awkwardness, or inviting rejection. A student who works skillfully in isolation, Rebecca is trying something new: making her own creative work visible to a peer, not just to an adult (her mom or her teacher). Her question to Grace ("Um, do you have a moment?") encompasses many purposes: from "Can you help me fulfill the conference expectation?" to more deeply: "Do you accept me?" "Am I safe?" "Will you value my writing, of which I am very proud?" "Can we be friends?" The intensity of the moment is felt not only by Rebecca but by Mr. Allegro and me as we watch. We feel for her shyness and hope she is not set back in the encounter. Flexible time and space have allowed Rebecca to move independently, with support, to choose her time and manner of approach. Her writing is integrated with emerging social tasks and abilities, developing a sense of membership with others. Small steps are necessary. Such "work" on Rebecca's part raises questions about whether classroom environments are shaped to support such encounters, and the extent to which social and emotional tasks are envisioned in the framing and design of the literacy curriculum.

Carla Finds Performance Partners

June 6, Year 1: I enter today and Carla immediately asks for help. She's finished the phone-call dialogue she started yesterday and wants approval to be able to recruit classmates for a sharing performance at the end of class. Mr. Allegro has let students know that not just any dialogue is eligible to share; they need to consult with an adult first.

As we sit at Carla's desk, the oscillating fan blows her papers to the floor. It's 85 degrees outside; the building is not air-conditioned. We decide to move to the idea station, where I invite Carla to read her dialogue to me as I look on. It starts with a big "RING RING" at the top of the page, followed by a conversation between two friends who have been trying out for a play. One didn't make it, and the other did. The first line of dialogue is: "So did you make the play . . . ?" The twist is that somebody sneezes loudly in the middle of the conversation, and both friends realize that there's an eavesdropper on the phone. An exchange follows in which a voice says, "But I'm big too!" The two-page dialogue ends with one of the girls saying, "See ya, I've got to go pound my little sister."

I'm entertained by the story, wondering momentarily about Carla's home life—does the story reflect an existing sibling relationship? Carla has written a script with all three parts, and, remarkably, has also composed two separate scripts with just the lines of the helping parts. Having multiple scripts is typically essential for performance, and Carla has gone out of her way to create these copies before other students are even on board. We work together first on her dialogue mechanics. Form and spelling are weaknesses for Carla, and at times it's unclear from the script who is speaking. After 7 minutes of editing together, I give her an okay.

Carla begins to search for performance partners. It's a big moment. She hasn't written this piece with others—so who will want to perform with Carla? She is relatively new to this 4th-grade group, and being the parent of a new 4th-grader myself, I am sensitive to her situation. Yesterday, I sat at lunch with a few students and overheard Carla talk about how she was teased last year, enough that she finally changed schools. She explained that the noticeable abrasions on her elbows this week came when someone knocked her down—intentionally, Carla felt—with a ball at recess. She is finding herself socially. Carla indicated to me, when we first sat down for our conference, that two girls she hoped to perform with—Jenna and

Naomi, both with relatively high status in the classroom—had already signaled that they were too busy today to perform a dialogue with her.

So Carla approaches Madeline. Madeline is easy-going and not one to hurt feelings. Carla also has already done Madeline a favor, going out of her way at lunch yesterday to ease the embarrassment when Madeline knocked over a pitcher of ice water. Carla announced publicly and graciously: "Oh, I'm always knocking things over at my house!" Indeed, my own son shared with me later his perception that Carla's reaction differed dramatically from the treatment boys typically receive from other boys when something similar happens. "They'd just be laughing . . ." he said.

But this time, Madeline declines. She's starting a new writing project regarding thank-you notes and wants to stick with it. Carla is momentarily crushed. She hangs her head, and I wonder how painful this process will be. With resilience, she heads to Missy, another lunch table partner for Carla. Missy, who has been somewhat reserved in class, took a lead part in a dialogue performance recently and has gained confidence before the group. To my own relief, Missy agrees to perform. Carla's social persistence has paid off, and her spirits are raised considerably; she needs one more partner. Ellen is walking out the door with Mr. Allegro for a conference, and Carla asks her quickly if she wants to join. Ellen listens and finally agrees when she realizes she can play the part of an "eavesdropper." In fact, Carla suddenly has a surplus of talent, as Ricky overhears the conversation and says: "Oh, I'm good at that. I can play the little brother!" He asks to see the script, which Carla shows him, but in the end Carla sticks with Ellen. Ricky would have been great in that part, but I'm also relieved that he can keep working on "Archie the Turtle." In the end, the rehearsal work among Carla, Missy, and Ellen, as they practice Carla's script for sharing time, is noticeably focused and engaged.

Commentary: What is revealed here about the intersection of Carla's social learning and writing growth? Carla seeks a way to build and nurture new relationships, and her phone dialogue functions directly as a "social" piece of writing. As a story, the dialogue itself allows classmates to imagine and process intense relational experiences, like making or not making the school play (a memorable experience for several students in Mr. Allegro's class this year), or managing a younger sibling amid new school friendships. Yet, the written dialogue not only depicts social experiences; it shapes relationships, or rather, it *is* a relationship in process—bringing peers together in performance, making literacy a shared enterprise of writing, reading, listening, and performing publicly. Carla's multiple scripts serve as concrete tools to reach across peer boundaries (she literally hands them to peers) and for creating social space for herself and others. Her approach, of course, is not foolproof. She experiences rejection along the way. Yet, writing is a powerful mediator, and Carla's scripts give her not only tools but confidence to persist. The phone dialogue is more than an imaginative writing product.

It functions as social mediation and invitation, creating a shared social reality, with real stakes, reflecting both social possibility and vulnerability for Carla and others in the class.

Such moments in workshop helped Mr. Allegro and me better acknowledge the relational processes many students were engaging in within the classroom through an open workshop setting. Growth in writing, in these cases, clearly overlapped with forms of social action—reaching out, assessing personal safety, reading another's needs, risk-taking, surviving a rejection, sharing about oneself. Workshop processes, such as the student-driven conference expectation, as well as the tools students themselves devised, such as Carla's dialogue scripts, mediated social experimentation and growth. Such social work helped us to perceive a wider set of tasks at work during writing time—particularly the need for connection—and to consider ways to support students accordingly.

NAVIGATING VOICE, CONTROL, AND STATUS

My second theme highlights interactions among writing partners, as they negotiated their relationships and friendships in and through writing events. I emphasize how writing together became an occasion for peers to experiment with and respond to different relational stances and power, especially as 4th-grade identities and connections were undergoing change. Students here reveal and engage in dynamics that consume significant emotional attention, as writing practices are intertwined with concerns about status and respect. Predictable issues surface; yet writing plays a crucial mediating role, serving as a mechanism for connection, marginalization, agency, and identity formation.

Such issues are often separated from literacy instruction and seen as part of a distinct "social-emotional curriculum" (Blad, 2015) or as related to systems of classroom management. Yet, in workshop, literacy development and social negotiation went hand in hand, as writing partnerships often became immersed in questions of voice, control, and status. These three terms became interrelated in workshop, as students faced issues of (1) whether they could "voice" or express what they wanted to in a writing partnership, (2) who had the power or control to steer the direction of a piece of writing, and (3) whether writing practices would support or detract from their own social status in the room. Workshop conditions (options for partnering, choice of topics, feedback systems, sharing time, and so on), I argue here, activated forms of social work in the presence of adults, giving students a chance to "work on" their social selves in a supported space. Being attentive to this dimension of writing, I argue further, expands the ways in which we might interpret students' learning and literacy development. I reflect first on a brief, tense interaction between Valerie and Gemma.

Telling the Truth, Feeling Eclipsed

March 3, Year 3: I check the hallway. Valerie and Gemma need assistance finding their file on the laptop. James, another student, overhears and helps them out, and they soon locate the file called "Giant Panda Story." In fact, this piece is not a story but an informational booklet, a nonfiction piece to help readers learn about a particular kind of bear that Valerie and Gemma love, giant pandas. I offer to type with them a bit, as they convert their hand-written draft into an electronic version. Valerie and Gemma have ranked their investment a "5" with this piece, the highest ranking (see Chapter 1 for a description of the rating system). They take time dictating paragraphs to me, as I sit on the floor next to them. I show them how to adjust the size of the text and title.

A bit of friction between these two is evident. They are both looking at their writing as they dictate, with Gemma holding the papers. As we work, Valerie suggests adding to a sentence Gemma has written. The sentence says that pandas "do not always fight invaders but sometimes just go by themselves." This is drawn from the research the girls have been doing about the often solitary nature of pandas in the wild. But Valerie has been reading further and has some additional information to offer; the information partly contradicts what Gemma has written. When Valerie shares her idea and suggests a wording change, Gemma says "No" with an edge in her voice. She pulls the paper quickly toward herself, indicating that she doesn't want to change what she has written. Valerie reacts, "Well, we should tell the truth!" Gemma isn't swayed, seeming to fear that her own voice in the piece will be eclipsed and/or that perhaps Valerie has too much power in their writing relationship. Valerie relents, with a bit of annoyance. They seem okay and focused, and I leave them to dictate the typing to each other. As I walk away, I ponder what I've seen and heard—namely, that ethical issues in writing, such as telling the truth, intersect with relationships and the desire for voice. This makes "truth" in writing, for me, more difficult to discern.

Commentary: Gemma and Valerie highlight a tension between truth, on the one hand, and relational recognition, on the other hand. Valerie seeks to improve the accuracy of their shared writing, yet Gemma asks not be eclipsed as a partner, not to be made invisible. Their interaction reminds me of team-teaching events in my own teacher education practice. I often ask graduate students to design and teach lessons with partners, and occasionally one candidate's desire to get a lesson "right" leads to "taking over" the lesson midstream, even during a peer's teaching turn, to make sure the lesson is "successful." Such taking over is always well intended, an effort to right the ship, but such moments are usually painful for the eclipsed partner, whose own opportunity to teach and learn has been appropriated.

Gemma and Valerie are negotiating a similar space, with Valerie leaning toward getting things right in the giant panda story by "telling the truth," as she puts it. It is a reasonable concern; she wants to be seen as knowledgeable, as a reliable student who is contributing new information to the work. Gemma, by contrast, seems to desire a space where her voice is clearly valued, not overshadowed. The latter concern is perhaps less appreciated in a traditional writing curriculum. Either way, the moment tests their friendship. Fortunately, they weather the conflict. Valerie yields to Gemma's needs, at least for the time being. Gemma, for her part, is learning to stand up for herself, to assert her voice, even as she must reflect on Valerie's assertion: "Well, we should tell the truth!" Both students must consider whether relying on factual "truth" is the only barometer of good writing (Nyberg, 1993; Smagorinsky, 1996). Both are learning how relationships influence writing and writing influences relationships.

Writing Partners, Creative Writing, and Borderline Bullying

Next, I offer a sequence of scenes that tracks the complex relationship between Jerry and his peers, particularly Hal, as they sought ways to negotiate voice, power, and status through the affordances of the workshop environment. Here, writing interactions with peers hinge less on issues of truth than on respect, appropriation, and marginalization in an evolving peer group.

January 14, Year 3: Jerry comes to me right at the start of workshop today to say that another student is borrowing his story idea. Jerry initiated "Superdog" in the first week of workshop, and it remains his focus. He uses a neutral voice but is clearly concerned:

"Nate is doing a Superdog story too," he says.

"Sounds like Superdog is a popular character," I reply.

Jerry and Nate sit by each other, and I soon hear Jerry bring up the issue to Nate directly. Jerry begins to offer Nate alternatives, such as maybe using a character called "Superbunny," but not Superdog. Nate responds, seemingly aware of the potential infringement and insisting that his Superdog will be different: It will have different powers and different characteristics. Listening, I sense that Nate is making a calculated choice, picking on Jerry, trying to get a rise out of him. But I am not sure. These are the first weeks of our workshop, and I don't know either student very well. Either way, Jerry senses violation. He keeps trying to move Nate into even a slightly modified title: "Why don't you try Mightydog rather than Superdog?" he asks plaintively. There is plenty of room here to talk about grown-up topics, like copyright, but I don't enter this terrain. I check in with Nate, who professes no ill will, and decide to move him to a different spot in the room. He promises to give his Superdog a distinct character profile.

January 27, Year 3: As workshop opens today, I soon notice Erik dictating to Hal some character detail: "a blue shirt," "an antenna sticking out of the top." Hal is writing this down on paper. He seems to be taking on the role of recorder or illustrator for Erik. Hal is content, serious, and soon working away on creating an image for Erik's story, "The Tick." I ask Hal how it's going. He tells me that he needed to take a break from his own "Normandy Invasion" paper, and he's going to illustrate for Erik for a while. Jerry picks up on this. A few minutes later, he brings some drawing ideas to Hal, saying aloud that Hal is "the best illustrator in the class." I caution Jerry about overloading Hal with work, which Jerry seems to respect, but he still moves over to the table with Hal. I'm away from these students for a while, and when I return, Jerry shows me a formal illustrator contract he has drawn up, actually signed by Hal. Hal has agreed to illustrate for "Superdog" as well. As I take in this development, I ask Jerry what Hal will get from the contract, and Hal speaks up: "Oh, I get to be mentioned on the cover and in the dedication."

February 3, Year 3: Hal is in the back corner, writing away. I wonder if he's starting a new piece, but he shows me some of Jerry's papers and tells me that he and Jerry are cowriting now, although Jerry is absent today. Hal has written a few sentences on a separate sheet, and his idea is to supplement Jerry's first chapter by giving a brief "backstory" to Superdog—that is, what happened between Superdog and his nemesis, the "Evil Leash," 10 years ago. This will serve as a kind of prologue, and he wants this to be included as the very beginning paragraph of Jerry's story. Hal seems quite immersed in Jerry's story, and his backstory concept is creative.

February 7, Year 3: Jerry asks to sit with me. We are a month into workshop. We read through the three chapters he and Hal have now apparently collaborated on. The story is coming together, but Jerry expresses concern. He is unhappy with the prologue. I ask if he wants Hal to join us for the conference, but Jerry says no. Jerry, as always, is polite and never directly accusatory, but the concern seems to be that Hal is taking over. We read Chapter 1, and Jerry says, "I don't think the police should just block off the bridge to keep people away from the fight between Superdog and Evil Leash" (Hal's idea); "The police should try to help Superdog out!" He wants to add dialogue: "Stop! Evil Leash. This is the police!" In many ways, these are useful additions, yet my intuition is that Jerry primarily wants to regain control over the story. After all, "Superdog" is his idea. As we work on these revisions to the prologue, Jerry reads aloud a sentence written by Hal, which includes a somewhat awkward double negative. I say incidentally, "That part might need some work." Jerry immediately turns to Hal, who is reading nearby, and says loudly enough for most students to hear: "Looks like you made a mistake, Hal!"

February 14, Year 3: Jerry has asked for another conference. The tension with Hal is high. Jerry again questions Hal's fight between the Evil Leash and Superdog in the prologue.

He says to me, "I don't like that they have a fight that occurred 100 years ago." Jerry mentions this aloud, so Hal, who is within earshot, can hear.

Hal chimes in, not looking up: "It's 10 years, not 100."

"But you said it was 100."

"Dogs don't live that long."

Hal's tone is deadpan and cutting. Jerry and I look at the story, and in fact, it says only 10 years. Jerry decides to change this to "17 years." When I ask Jerry to read the section to me, he calls Hal over, but Hal declines. Jerry's recent conferences are designed to help him gain authorship back, so Hal stays away.

Jerry remains vulnerable. His status in peer relationships seems uncertain, and he becomes at times a social target, particularly with the male peers in this class with whom he most wants to be friends. Jerry feels this, is insecure about it, and his peers play out the dynamic. Behind me, I hear teasing among Erik, Hal, and Shaun about Jerry.

Shaun, who struggles with writing himself, comes over to Jerry and asks, "So, how did Superdog get his powers?" Jerry says he doesn't know, but then declares brightly, "Maybe he was born in a dinosaur egg!" He smiles and laughs at his own idea. The other three, listening, laugh, too— but at Jerry, not with him. As Mr. Allegro announces sharing time, Jerry raises his hand excitedly. Hal shakes his head to himself and says quietly, sarcastically, "Jerry, no."

February 14, continued: Sharing time: Mr. Allegro calls on a few students before finally acknowledging Jerry, who comes up front. I watch for the reactions of the other boys. As Jerry begins to face his classmates, however, Hal surprisingly steps up and joins him—not what I expected. He stands by Jerry, apparently not wanting to miss the limelight. It's an interesting shift. Hal's connection with Jerry is complex—sometimes caring and friendly, other times opportunistic, at times bordering on bullying. Yet, Jerry's story is catchy and somewhat popular with the class. Hal doesn't want to miss out. He is a coauthor, after all. The draw of sharing time is powerful.

Jerry starts out, speaking for both of them: "As you know, Hal and I wrote this story about Superdog, but Hal has a little problem with it." Jerry alludes to their conflict over the prologue but doesn't elaborate. As he prepares to read, one student says, "Read from the beginning!" But Jerry says, "We just want to read Chapter 3." He starts, getting lost a few times in the writing, and Hal whispers words and gently points to the page to assist, keeping Jerry on track. Jerry finishes, then smiles and says, "Today we got a comment on our story—about how Superdog was formed." Shaun, who has been drawing intently during sharing time and had earlier teased Jerry, stops and looks up. Jerry continues: "My idea is that he was hatched from dinosaur eggs." This gets a murmur from the class, and Hal quickly adds: "That was *his* idea." Several students chuckle. But Jerry seems okay with this, and the overall classroom mood is light. Moreover, the question sponsors real discussion among students. A few comments follow, probing for plausibility: Jackie asks, "How could he come from a dinosaur egg if all dinosaurs were extinct in the ice age?" Another says, "How did he live after the meteor?" Jerry answers, taking each question seriously, and referring back to a fictional TV show where, apparently, a dinosaur egg was preserved in ice and kept alive until the present day.

Commentary: Jerry is vulnerable to derision and poaching from his peers, in a complex relationship that moves on multiple levels from friendship to thinly veiled bullying. Poaching occurs as Nate begins a parallel Superdog story, which he pursues even as he sees that it is hurtful to Jerry. Somewhat like Carla, Jerry seeks out peers, especially Hal, for relational connection, classroom status, and writing support, but he also must resist incursion, as even friends, like Hal, are driven to take over Jerry's creative space. The preoccupation with Superdog, at least for Jerry's male friends, seems to be less about the story itself or the quality of its writing traits and more about social purposes and positioning. Especially central seems to be the task of keeping Jerry off balance, actively maintaining a kind of social marginalization. Jerry's story itself becomes a bargaining chip, one that Jerry uses to try to increase his social stock in the room—and that his friends conversely manipulate to keep Jerry from rising too high.

Purposeful forms of writing, like the contract, emerge spontaneously as students engage their social needs and positioning. Ostensibly about Hal's drawing abilities, the contract also keeps Jerry connected to Hal's relatively high status in the room. Responding to my question about what Hal "gets" from the contract arrangement, Hal quickly names specific forms of writing as compensation—that is, that Jerry's published work will have a "cover page" and "dedication," where Hal's illustrations can be publicly acknowledged. The contract itself is both impressive and telling. Complete with signature, it binds Hal to Jerry, reflecting in a way Jerry's vulnerability and need for security, as if just *asking* Hal for help would not be enough. Later, sensing a loss of control over his story, Jerry uses writing conferences with adults to reassert his authorship and position. To gain ground, he unceremoniously points out flaws in Hal's writing. Writing forms and practices thus mediate relationships in a delicate balance of connection, power, status, and creativity.

Several researchers (Rodkin, 2004; Smith, 2010,) suggest that bullying in upper elementary school reflects responses to institutional structures, especially the shift that students anticipate in moving from more intimate and protected elementary worlds (with a single, designated, caretaking adult) to larger, more bureaucratic middle school spaces characterized by less personal caretaking and with power being to a greater extent "up for grabs" among students. On the brink of this significant shift, Hal, Jerry, and their peers experiment with multiple stances and strategies in managing relationships. Hal floats among different roles—friend, illustrator, critic, bully, and gentle supporter—stances that fluctuate depending on the writing circumstance. Hal exerts power, for example, moving from illustrator to substantially rewriting Jerry's opening chapter. This act seems to reflect competing desires: both to genuinely help Jerry with the story and also to steal some of Jerry's thunder—to keep Jerry, in effect, under control. Hal scorns, with other boys, Jerry's desire to share an idea about the origins of Superdog with the whole class, assuming that it will be embarrassing. But moments later, Hal stands with Jerry and gently helps him read before the group, softening his tone playfully ("That was *his* idea"), which Jerry doesn't take as mean-spirited. The two find a way back together.

Shaun, similarly, baits and makes fun of Jerry's idea on the origins of Superdog in one moment, but in the next Shaun is listening as several students in the class take the idea seriously and pose questions about it in class. These shifts in stance and role make visible the complexity and permeability of upper elementary social worlds. Students do not live out fixed identities or social roles, such as simply defined "friends," "bullies," or "victims." Even though Jerry seems more vulnerable socially, the students move in and out of various roles and positions, and they use the available writing tasks to manage their changing relationships. Writing and social interaction are interwoven, and multiple factors—including adult feedback—influence student perception, experience, and response to inclusion and exclusion. Students are open to tremendous growth and change.

Issues of voice, control, and status played out with intensity, at times, in workshop, providing adults with insight into rich interpersonal dynamics and broadening our view of what students need as learners. Jerry, for example, is marginalized but not powerless in these scenes—and he may need and desire, above all, a way for writing partnerships to embody fully cooperative relationships, where partners aim to support one another's perspective, ideas, and needs, rather than competing for status or poaching ideas in zero sum fashion. This may be a learning zone for Jerry and his peers, one that influences the way adults shape future shared writing opportunities, name dynamics, and respond to issues that arise. Flexibly structured writing contexts, I argue here, provide a means for making visible, and for engaging, such realities in upper elementary lives. Writers' workshop allowed students to experiment with voice and agency from multiple positions and with new tools—and gave adults opportunities to shape and engage a social curriculum.

EMBRACING THE SOCIAL (WRITING) CURRICULUM

In classrooms, a logic of "expected outcomes" often divides us from the present moment—focusing attention on the future, on hoped-for writing outcomes—separating content from social worlds. Relational impulses are too often framed as distractions to be monitored or tolerated, as an extracurricular reality that takes "management" on our part. We may learn to use groups and grouping strategies, but purely or primarily as a means for increasing academic learning and literacy. The content curriculum remains central, above, and separate from the social. Relational work in schools—developing a social identity, working through social tensions, navigating status, becoming a friend—is prevalent, but often sidelined. In the scenes above, by contrast, I illustrate ways in which relational work was a central, consistent dimension of student experience during writing workshop, part of the "assemblage" of writing. For economy, I have highlighted just two areas—students building social connections with one another and navigating voice, control, and status. I have emphasized how flexible writing practices not only revealed social worlds and needs, but also mediated relational work, providing space for reaching out, trying on new identities, engaging status hierarchies and exclusion, and offering tools for agency, affiliation, and voice.

Such dynamics were highly motivating for students, a locus of heightened energy. As Dyson (2013) discovered in a study of two classrooms of primary age writers, "even the least experienced composers were interested in writing as a means of social connection" (p. 170). At the upper elementary level, student energy was often tied to affiliation and social positioning, as both played out through writing. Gemma's emotions rose as she perceived her own voice being eclipsed, leading to a charged exchange with Valerie—the entire sequence immersed within their shared passion to depict the lives of giant pandas. Carla's bid for performance partners was filled with disappointment and elation, as she intermixed a writing initiative with relationship building. Jerry and Hal rode a roller coaster of evolving intensity, of exclusion and inclusion, as "Superdog" became a site for managing changing social realities in 4th grade. In this respect, "affective intensities" (Leander & Boldt, 2012) do not simply involve romantic or positive emotions, but instead reveal where student energy lies in the moment, signaling ways in which children are individually and collectively *present*—helping us see a broader experiential field through which learning occurs.

Attention to relational energies does not mean that we ignored actual student writing, writing processes, or discrete skills. But in some ways, it called into question what actual writing is, and what writing "processes" are. We might ask, for example: What processes, or whose processes, are most central to Jerry and Hal's development in cowriting "Superdog"? To what extent can their writing skills be disassociated from the relational imperatives described above? What about with Carla's script writing? To what extent does a usual focus on individual production, outcome, and assessment miss or ignore relational "becomings" that may be at the very center of student writing? Such questions push back against our usual assumption that writing is taught in linear fashion, with the teacher and the content separate from the learner as a "higher organizing principle" (Olsson, 2009, p. 74), and the writer as an individual receiver of skills, acting out designated processes.

Such a critique doesn't tell us precisely "what to do" as teachers, but it might help us keep Carla's relational instincts in mind as she develops her performance dialogue, even if her conventions need work. If we perceive Carla's scripts to be entangled with a desire to make connections in a new 4th-grade community, we might seek ways to support this quest and its "power to continue" (Dahlberg & Moss, 2009, p. xxii). Such a stance might likewise lead us into new territory with Gemma and Valerie as they engage the merits of "telling the truth." We might, for example, rethink simplistic binary divisions such as "fact" versus "opinion"—and consider students' relational needs as they decide what to include and exclude in their writing. Such a commitment might further help us track the delicate ground that Jerry and Hal are on, possibly leading to guidance and problem solving. As adults, we might come to see our roles less as regulating social activities that interfere with writing and more in terms of "a pedagogy of listening" (Dahlberg, 2003), one that attends to multifaceted writing realities.

These were areas of growth for Mr. Allegro and me. We did not begin our workshop emphasizing relational work among students. We were more focused on a fairly limited conception of "writing" itself. Social impulses and issues, and their role in writing, emerged as a discovery or surprise once we had altered the landscape, just as Martin's video game screen shots were a surprise (see Chapter 2), opening our perspective about what becoming a writer might mean. Such events emerged on their own, influencing writing tasks and motivations in less-than-predictable ways. Yet, they illuminated intersections of writing and relational growth, with adults positioned to observe, listen, and guide. Indeed, upper elementary teachers have pragmatic work to do around issues of power, marginalization, and potential eruptions of bullying culture. The writing environment we created did not eliminate such issues. Rather, it allowed them to become visible with and amid the curriculum, rather than segregated from it. It immersed us as adults *in* such issues, and it raised questions about the extent to which our conceptions of curriculum might better account for social and emotional growth, alongside writing, with elementary learners.

QUESTIONS FOR REFLECTION

- Thinking of your own students, or your own experiences, to what extent might energy and motivation for writing reside in and be shaped by interactions with others?
- How would you characterize the growth occurring for Grace and Carla as they reach out to other students with their writing?
- What specific roles or steps would you take in supporting Jerry and Hal as they navigate issues of status and control in writing?
- What do you find most intriguing, or challenging, about the mutual interconnections between writing and relationships?
- How might teachers capture the effects of a listening stance—recording, valuing, and/or using relational observations to inform everyday teaching and learning?

CHAPTER 5

Sharing and Publishing

Being Seen, Heard, and Valued

Acts of sharing and publishing writing are identity-shaping forces. Interacting with audiences, making one's writing visible to others, involves excitement, purpose, and risk, shaping how students come to regard themselves, and one another, as writers and learners in classrooms. Faced with real audiences, grounded in their own motivations, public sharing in writers' workshop helped students make sense of writing as purposeful communication. They confronted not only questions of writing clarity and proficiency, but fundamental issues of validation and membership in the classroom. In this chapter, I argue that flexible norms and the acceptance of self-directed goals propelled many students to make their writing public, that is, to share writing openly with classmates. Indeed, as students engaged with immediate audiences, their language creativity and responsiveness grew. Yet, public sharing also placed students in vulnerable positions. Adult assumptions about sharing, and how such events unfolded, were of crucial importance and often seemed to influence writer identities—that is, the extent to which students saw themselves as positively connected to writing practices. Our adult stance and approach determined whether students could experience themselves as full members of the classroom community.

Writing became "public" in Mr. Allegro's classroom in a few ways. At the end of nearly every session, student volunteers were invited to come forward and read or talk about writing in progress. Mr. Allegro facilitated. We designated a stool at the front of the class, one that Mr. Allegro sometimes used to sit on while teaching, as the "author's chair." Students could come forward and sit, or they would simply stand next to the stool, as they read their work aloud or shared a publication. We emphasized that sharing time was not about finished or perfect products; it was primarily for trying out one's writing before others, seeing how peers might respond, and taking a few questions.

Graves and Hansen (1983) assert that an author's chair is an essential component in classrooms where children learn to "play their way into an understanding of reading and writing" (p. 178). Sharing writing, in this view, is a kind of "play," as students essentially try on new roles and social positions with one another through language. Through ritually designated sharing, children gradually take on a sense of authorship and agency, specifically as they "both exercise and experience the effects of audience" (p. 181). An author's chair also enables the interconnectedness of reading and writing. Students learn that "their responsibility as a writer is to anticipate questions from readers. Their responsibility as a reader is to ask question[s] of authors" (p. 182). Through sharing aloud and engaging an audience, students not only come to take on the identity of a writer as someone with something to say, but they also develop "option awareness" (p. 180)—the idea that they, and others, might be able to write and say things *differently*. Mr. Allegro and I hoped to cultivate such awareness through regular sharing practices.

A second way of making writing public, in contrast to oral sharing, was through publishing. Publishing, in many ways, was a physical activity. When the conferencing process was complete and a piece was ready for publication, we would help students select, measure, and trim a cover page, then use a binding machine to punch holes and attach a binding strip. Students were encouraged to design the cover, include a dedication, and/or create an "about the author" page. Approval for publication was usually determined by Mr. Allegro, with input from volunteers. We looked for writers to have challenged themselves in light of feedback received and based on individual goals and abilities. (See my struggle with such approval in working with Angel and Isabel in Chapter 3.)

Mr. Allegro would normally acknowledge any new publication during that day's sharing time, giving students a chance to read or tell about their published work. Publishing, thus, often overlapped with sharing before the class, though it was more focused on celebration and validation than on feedback. Mr. Allegro displayed student publications on magazine shelves in the classroom, and students were invited to read or review these works if they were interested. Overall, we framed publishing as a *possible* outcome for writers, rather than an expectation or requirement, to avoid undue pressure; we did not want students to feel that they "had" to publish. Still, publishing took on unique energy because of the public recognition received—and it became a motivating force in the room.

With either sharing or publishing routines, we sought to create a public space that was democratic—that is, open to a wide range of community strengths, abilities, perspectives, and motivations. Some classroom observers express concern that even in workshop settings, public sharing is sometimes reconfigured to meet adult goals rather than student needs. Describing her work with elementary teachers using writing workshops in a large metropolitan city, McCallister (2008) writes that "the implicit message across the practice literature is that the Author's Chair . . . should be utilized to reinforce the teacher's instructional agenda that takes shape in the form of direct application of isolated conventions or techniques. . . " (p. 461). Public sharing, thus, becomes "the opportunity for teachers to showcase successful examples of writing from children who have followed the teacher's instructions" (p. 461). For some, this is commonsense teacher practice; yet others point out that under such conditions, the learning strengths, needs, and attempts of diverse language learners can be withdrawn from view. Sharing time becomes less about trying out language in an exploratory form and finding one's own footing; writer experimentation is ignored. Genishi (2016) argues that when formal goals and expectations (where students "should" be) begin to overtake a teacher's sense of what kids are actually doing or are able to do, students experience a "mismatch" (p. 150) in the literacy curriculum, placing them at risk.

The scenes below focus on the ways in which learning to write in our workshop was entwined with "being seen, heard, and valued." Sharing and publishing events gave students avenues to make their literacy impulses, needs, and desires visible—and, through the eyes of peers and adults, to understand themselves, and writing itself, in new ways. The scenes, all from the first year of workshop, are sequenced chronologically. In the first set of scenes, from March, I describe how students *were drawn into* public spaces, an experience that typically cycled them back into and through their own writing, promoting innovation and language development. In the second set of scenes, from May, I track the strategic moves of two students as they carefully *negotiate exposure and recognition* before the class. In the third set of scenes, from June, I highlight how sharing and publishing *generated membership* for potentially marginalized students. In all, the scenes represent various ways in which writing identities and language experiences were shaped through access to visible public spaces in the classroom.

THE LURE OF PUBLISHING

Jenna and Madeline Try out Publishing

March 13, Year 1: Jenna approaches me and says, "I'm ready to publish my book." I look at her papers. She has a typed version of her story, newly printed, although I notice that the formatting is off. Her second chapter starts at the very bottom of a mostly blank page.

Jenna seems to be motivated by other newly published stories in workshop, such as Vanni's "The Three Little Cats" and Hope's "Madison the Mummy." These are now displayed on a magazine shelf. Interestingly, Vanni's and Hope's writings stand at opposite ends of a traditionally conceived spectrum of writing ability. Vanni's story, a simple remake of "The Three Little Pigs," was the first celebrated publication, although as an English language learner, his writing is among the least assured in the class. We've announced and celebrated each publication, which has led to a kind of status revolution for Vanni. He told me today, as I showed Jenna how we can get each chapter to start on a new page: "Oh, I know what you're doing. You're going to publish. My story was the first one to publish."

With her formatting in better shape, Jenna locates two pieces of red construction paper for the cover. I've only used the binder once, so Jenna, who has apparently used the device before, gives me advice throughout the process, like that I should punch all the pages together and not in sections so that all the holes for the binding clip will line up evenly. Fortunately, the binding works, and a red cover surrounds her story, with a narrow black plastic clip clasping the pages together. Voilà! A "book" is created. This is an exciting moment.

Next, I work with Madeline. She is going through her writing folder and takes out a story she completed last month but chose not to publish. She had rated it a "2" out of 5 then, but now she thinks it might be a "4," which signals that she is "very interested" in this work and wants "to keep developing it" (see Chapter 1 for a description of the rating system). I recognize the story as a creative, 12-page, diary-based narrative, which Madeline has titled "Nanina." The story takes place in India in the 1600s and relays a fictional series of events in the voice of a princess's servant. Madeline's writing is engaging and imaginative, and I'm glad she has finally decided that she likes "Nanina." I ask her if she is thinking of publishing the story now, but she says no, because "typing it would take too long." I let Madeline know that her story really doesn't *need* to be typed. Handwritten stories used to be the only kind published, I tell her. She hesitates, looks through the pages, and says that there are too many cross-outs and revision arrows on the existing version. These are written in pencil, based on conferencing she has done weeks before with adults. I say, "Madeline, I think you can just clean this up a bit with your eraser." I realize that I am actively encouraging her to publish—and perhaps that my desire for her to publish, in this moment, exceeds her own. But she seems intrigued with the process, and I'm not sure that Madeline realizes how good "Nanina" is. My sense is that Madeline will enjoy having a published piece and that her classmates may benefit from having access to her creativity. She finally agrees.

As Madeline makes her final changes, Jenna has been basking in her own publication. During sharing time today, Mr. Allegro invites Jenna to read from her newly finished book. She sits on the stool before the class. The title of her story, "The Great Summer," is now written in black marker on the red cover page. She reads a paragraph. The section recounts her family's camping trip, especially how her little brother ate all the marshmallows, graham crackers, and chocolate they'd brought with them on the very first day. She describes the camp showers and how cold the water was. Mr. Allegro asks the class if many of them have gone camping. Several raise their hands, and a few laugh about cold showers. We then discuss what kind of story Jenna's is. During sharing time, we've been trying to name specific genres that are emerging in the classroom. When a new type appears, we write the genre name on an orange sheet of construction paper and post it on a classroom wall. Our goal is to make visible a variety of forms and to encourage diverse writing possibilities. Jenna responds first, calling "The Great Summer" a "true story." But she then admits that it didn't really happen to her. She says the story happened to someone else while she went camping. She says she wrote the story *as if* it had happened to her. After some discussion, most students believe the story should be designated "Based on a True Story."

After class, Madeline is ready with "Nanina," and we go to the binding room, and Madeline's friend Alana joins us. Alana is ready to publish a new SpongeBob story. Both are happy to forfeit their recess time. Madeline wants purple construction paper for her cover; Alana wants beige. Tomorrow, their job will be to design the covers, adding titles, names, perhaps an illustration, and maybe pasting a dedication page inside. Madeline has already published other work, but as we leave the binding room, she holds up the bound story and says aloud, "My first handwritten publication." (See Figure 5.1.)

March 14, Year 1: The next day, Madeline's and Alana's stories are standing on the magazine rack, their title pages nicely designed, facing out to the class. They have completed the final touches outside of workshop. Vanni comes by the display and checks in with his own story, "The Three Little Cats." Mr. Allegro relays to me that Vanni now walks over and touches the green cover of his story at least two to three times each day. As Vanni stands by the publications, he grabs Alana's new work, titled "SpongeBob Squarepants: Legend of the Golden Spatula," reading it aloud as he stands next to me. He reads fluently, with inflection and voice, asking me occasionally for help with a few words, like *partner*. Vanni says aloud, "This is good!" and continues to read.

During sharing time, Madeline comes up to the author's chair with her published story. She has now added a preface, which sits inside the cover page. It reads: "This is a story of a girl named Nanina. She works for Jahnara, the princess of India. They have fun together. Even when . . ." After sharing this preface, she reads aloud her newly written dedication:

Deticated to Alana for being my inspiration.
By cutting her hair she looks like the main charater.
Also because she was the first person to read my book.

Madeline then reads one of Nanina's diary entries. After the reading, Mr. Allegro asks Madeline what kind of story or genre this is. Madeline pauses and then says, "It's sort of historical fiction," but then says, "it's also a journal!" Mr. Allegro says maybe it represents a genre we haven't talked about yet: "fictional journal." Madeline seems happy with this.

Figure 5.1. Excerpt from Madeline's Story, "Nanina" (Text Below)

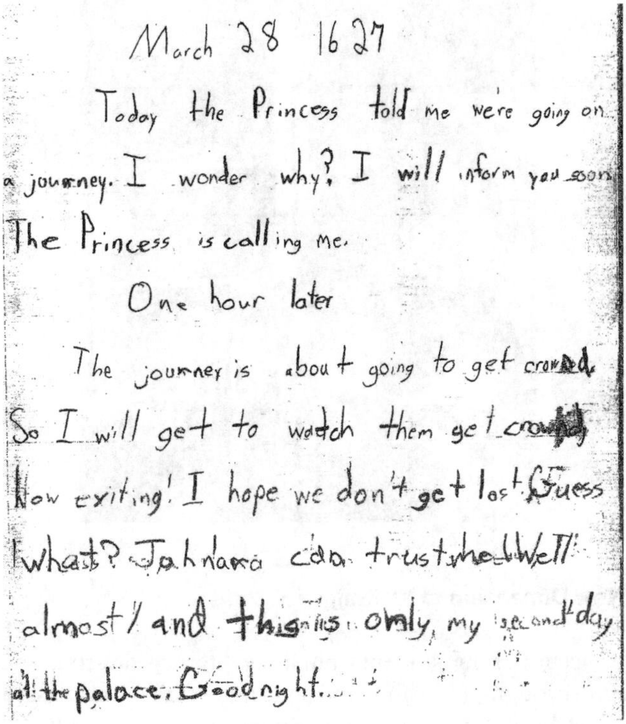
March 28 1627

Today the Princess told me were going on a journey. I wonder why? I will inform you soon. The Princess is calling me.

One hour later

The journey is about going to get crownd. So I will get to watch them get crownd. How exiting! I hope we don't get lost. Guess what? Jahnara can trust me. Well almost / and this is only my second day at the palace. Goodnight.

Today the Princess told me we're going on a journey. I wonder why? I will inform you soon. The Princess is calling me. One hour later the journey is about going to get crownd [crowned]. So I will get to watch them get crownd, how exiting [exciting]! I hope we don't get lost. Guess what? Jahnara can trust me. Well almost / and this is only my second day at the palace. Goodnight.

Finally, Hope, Naomi, Jenna, Serena, and Eliza arise to present a play that Hope has written and directed. It's a two-page play about girls who get trapped by a witch—a story that Hope says is based on Hansel and Gretel. The students have spent the past 2 days making props for the performance, and they used 15 minutes of workshop today to rehearse. Now, Hope watches carefully as the other girls enact her play before the class, each with her own copy of the script. It begins with Naomi: "Today is SO boring . . ." Most of these girls just finished a week working with a drama group after school—their acting skills are keen. The drama experience has induced Hope to compose the play and the girls to want to put it on. They are completely in a flow of engagement. Dante, however, gets frustrated with their stops, restarts, and giggles and calls the performance "horrible." Partly, he's frustrated as the class has inadvertently gone 3 minutes into lunch time.

Figure 5.2. Publication Shelf

Adding a New Dimension to Writing

These brief scenes show students pursuing literacy desiring and language development through publishing and sharing events in the classroom. Jenna and Madeline, both confident writers, initiate steps to publish their work. They anticipate and experience the effects of audience. The display shelf itself (see Figure 5.2.) has taken on value—as a means of recognition—and as a relevant, palpable outcome for students' writing efforts. Mr. Allegro and I have tried to maintain the display as a space of celebration without letting it become a stigma for those who choose not to publish. We do this, however successfully, by not over-valorizing the shelf and by emphasizing its functionality—that is, as an addition to the classroom library, offering material for reading and examples of possible student writing.

Overall, public space adds a new dimension and infuses energy into writing experiences, placing students in newfound social relations with others and sending them back into their own language. Jenna's desire to publish sets in gear a series of formatting decisions to meet her audience's needs. Sharing her work before the class kindles a simple but important discussion of genre—on the difference between "true story" and "based on a true story." Madeline is driven to reread her collection of writing. Over time, she gains new perspective on the quality of "Nanina," assessing its readiness for a wider audience. The fact that the story is "handwritten," which she initially sees as a limitation, becomes an asset. Madeline also uses the publishing opportunity to generate new, purposeful writing—a brief synopsis with a suspenseful question, such as we might find on the outside of a book jacket, as well as a dedication to Alana, which Madeline reads aloud in a public gesture of friendship.

Opportunities for sharing and publication motivate a range of literacy initiatives among students. Vanni, a new language learner, and our first workshop publisher, mingles with classmates at the display shelf, taking up and reading the available writing of his peers. The publication shelf, and Vanni's own published book, draw him into a circle of literacy-related relationships. Reading a classmate's book, he integrates reading, writing, and speaking. He confers an accolade on a classmate's writing. He experiences confidence and membership, even as a potentially vulnerable student amid a wide range of language skills in the classroom. For Hope and her story, the "author's chair" is something of a misnomer, with its implied sense of a single author, sitting down, reading. In this case, Hope takes on the role of "director," standing to the side, as the author's chair becomes a "stage" for a band of friends to embody her script. Public sharing fuels literacy desiring. Drama, writing, friendships, physical space, materials (props, scripts), and audience recognition come together—driving creativity, communication, motivation, and a sense of purpose among students.

NEGOTIATING PUBLIC SPACES

Ava Creates a Mini-Sharing Event

May 22, Year 1: Near the end of today's session, I ask Ava if I can read part of her writing. She is reluctant, tells me it's "weird," but then agrees. Ava is a solitary though highly engaged writer in our workshop. She dives deep into her work, composing for extended periods of time, though she seldom shares her writing with others. She has a quiet friendship with Brendan, a boy who sits next to her. By this time in the year, each has produced, and continues to work on, an extended piece of writing. Ava's is a quirky fantasy fiction piece tied to video and television characters. Brendan is telling the story of "General B," a futuristic intergalactic narrative that begins in the year 5702.

Mr. Allegro starts sharing time before I've read much of Ava's writing, and I put it aside as students begin. There are many volunteers today. Jenna and Naomi provide another installment in a saga about "summer school." Serena likewise gives us the very latest of her story about the crazed "Maxwell." Eliza reads her new piece called "My Russian Snail"—just three lines of writing. We pass around a tiny drawing of a snail that Eliza has created. Neil then stands and reads his new piece about a "game cube" he has that relates to computers. After this, Naomi asks, "What kind of story is that?" Mr. Allegro fields the question, a good one, because Neil's work is not narrative but a description of a technology he is interested in. Mr. Allegro asks Neil what kind of writing he thinks it is, and when he's quiet, another student offers an idea: "True story." Then Alana raises her hand and suggests, "Magazine article?" Public sharing elicits these tentative, but interesting, considerations of genre.

Class ends. Ava comes over as I return to her notebook. She has a mature story-world, full of voice and writing invention. The part I read focuses on a character, Pierce, who is watching TV and bored senseless as he clicks through various channels. The narration weaves back and forth between sounds ("click-click"), mock TV voices, and Ava's narrator voice. There are inside references and jokes that I don't follow very well. I begin to read aloud with Ava next to me. Hearing my attempts, she realizes I have the tone wrong. She spontaneously takes over the reading aloud, taking the story in her own hands and giving voice to her own story, using the "right" voicing and inflection. She creates a mini-sharing event of her own, though only after class has ended. "Oh, now I get it," I say, as she finishes reading. "That's great." Ava quickly explains a subtle joke that I missed, then is off to recess.

Brendan Finds a Way to Publish

May 29, Year 1: Brendan, Ava's compatriot, tells me his "Book of Drawings" is ready to publish. This work surprises me, because for weeks and weeks Brendan has been diligently working on "General B," which we affectionately call his masterpiece. I've assumed he would be finalizing "General B." I look over the "Book of Drawings." It has a series of simple, full-page pencil sketches, with brief titles near the bottom, all related to popular movies or video games, such as *Star Wars* and Legend of Zelda (see Figure 5.3). Brendan tells me about the pictures, which are a bit hard for me to understand. Given the extended effort he's put into "General B," this seems a bit thrown together. Brendan says he thinks it's ready to be published.

"What's become of 'General B'?" I ask. He says he just wanted to work on some new drawings. Pushing a bit, I ask if the drawings are organized the way he wants, and if he wants to write anything more for his audience, perhaps clarifying his goals and why he wrote it. I say, "Sometimes a writer can help readers make sense of things, so they don't have to guess so much." Brendan has little to say. I suggest a table of contents. He looks at me blankly. I am trying to discern his motivation. He has been working hard to finish his "General B" story. It is an extended piece, and the amount of work has possibly been overwhelming. He's stopped, I suspect, just to have *something* published, as if he's found a creative way to take a break, try something new, and still motivate himself.

I say, "Well, sometimes books can allow the reader to do more guessing—is that what you want here?" Brendan nods. I fear I'm making the act

Figure 5.3. "Book of Drawings" Excerpt

The legend of
Zelda

of publication too easy, and yet, given his enormous efforts with "General B," perhaps the opposite is the case—that publishing or even finishing his masterpiece has, in fact, become too difficult. Brendan needs a more accessible route. To solve the problem, he borrows from Carla's recent "Idea Book" concept (see Chapter 2) with a mostly visual publication.

I help Brendan find construction paper for his cover, and he works on the title. Looking things over, there is more complexity in the work than I had originally seen: The images are thoughtfully conceived and detailed, sometimes funny. There are interesting pairings—a pair of drawings from *Star Wars*, a pair on Legend of Zelda, a pair on something called "Thumb Wars," which seems to be a pun on the *Star Wars* pair. Brendan completes a dedication page to Ava, his faithful writing partner. He thanks her "for helping me at thinking of what to draw." Brendan and I then head down the hallway and finish the binding process. Back in class, I ask if he wants to place his story up on the publication shelf, but he says instead, "Mr. Allegro usually says a few things about the published stories, so I think I'll keep it here for now." The importance of his "Book of Drawings" comes into view. Brendan doesn't just want to have something on the display shelf or take a break from "General B"; he wants to be recognized before the class and be talked about by his teacher. This is perhaps especially important, given the late date in the semester. It's getting down to the wire for being recognized as a published author.

Come sharing time, Jenna and Naomi, first to volunteer, read a section that includes a boy kissing a girl on the cheek, with the comment, "I only kiss the people I hate." This is a masterful line of 4th-grade dialogue. It elicits intrigued looks on faces around the classroom. Next, Serena reads from her work about kids who are orphaned after their parents commit suicide. Sharing time, for some students, has become an opportunity to update the class on the newest developments in tantalizing, edgy narratives, like installments in serial magazines.

At the end, Mr. Allegro remembers to celebrate the new publication. He announces that Brendan now has a "Book of Drawings" and invites him to the front. Brendan rises, mentioning bashfully that his book actually has very little writing, almost as if he doesn't want the attention. He goes to the front and stands before the class. When invited, he says he doesn't want to read or share anything. After holding up the cover to show the group and waiting a moment, he walks to the corner shelf and places his story with the other publications. Though it is an understated moment, I know this means a great deal to him.

Showing Agency with Sharing Structures

In these vignettes, Ava and Brendan, two friends, confident in themselves though often reserved in the social space of the classroom, find their own ways of sharing and receiving recognition. Both students are very much into the workshop, developing lengthy, creative pieces. They stick together and support each other but they rarely share writing openly.

Working with my invitation to read her work, Ava maneuvers in and around sharing time, managing to have her writing voice heard. Even as she composes with intensity each session, she is cautious about placing her writing before others, let alone before the entire group. Yet, as she hears me read her work aloud—soon after hearing Jenna, Naomi, and Serena share—she is compelled to take over the event, creating her own impromptu oral sharing, well after formal sharing is over. She doesn't take my faulty reading as a sign that her writing needs improvement. Rather, for Ava, her writing needs someone who knows *how* to read it, who *gets* the narrative enough to be able to pull off its sophistication. Ava is learning about the space between what is written and how something might be read—about the "sound" of her writing, about interactions of voice and audience. In relation to our sharing time structure, however, Ava asserts agency in *how* she learns such lessons. Even as she takes large steps with voice in her writing, she needs smaller, nuanced steps to embody that voice for others.

Brendan likewise negotiates literacy in a public space, yet with a different desire. His "Book of Drawings" is a seeming sidetrack in his writing process. He breaks off from the expected pathway (to keep writing "General B") to pursue public validation from his teacher. Even as adults have been impressed by his strong commitment and writing stamina, by his lengthy, creative efforts with "General B," and by his willingness to take feedback, we also may have missed something. Brendan needs recognition for all that he is doing as a writer, even though his masterpiece may not get finished. Brendan is not a needy student by any means. Rather, in workshop, he draws upon a range of components to sustain engagement—a friendship with Ava, an interest in futuristic space stories, visual images, and in this case, a structure for public validation. A quiet, consistent presence in the classroom, Brendan desires *assurance* as we near the end of the workshop, validation that he's been a contributing member of the community.

To an extent, I wonder if our publishing celebrations exert undue pressure on students—pushing Brendan, for example, to seek out recognition simply because he has felt left out. Yet I am even more impressed by how students like Ava and Brendan interact creatively *with* our sharing structures, bending them to their needs. The fact that workshop supports a wide range of writing possibilities gives both students ways to be seen and heard on their own terms.

SHAPING COMMUNITY MEMBERSHIP

Martin Publishes a Collection

June 5, Year 1: Over the past few weeks, Martin, who has invested great energy in video game drawings throughout workshop (see Chapter 2), has been moving toward publication. Taking up a volunteer's suggestion, he has decided to compile his work into a "collection." Drawing continues to be central to Martin's composing, although his confidence with alphabetic writing has increased significantly. Recently, he produced an entire page of print about a monster/deity named Trydus (see Figure 5.4). Through workshop, Martin's output has been prodigious, and his corpus of writing reflects his knowledge and interests as well as exacting levels of detail. Writing and drawing have emerged in concert.

The very notion of a "collection" is an unexpected outcome, something we hadn't anticipated. As a publication concept, it differs from what has been produced so far. Students have published single works around a storyline (like Jenna's "The Great Summer") or concept (like Brendan's "Book of Drawings"). Martin's work, by contrast, is a kind of portfolio, a compilation of favorite drawings, stories, and even a few jokes he has heard and illustrated. Once the idea of a collection emerged (a suggestion from a parent volunteer), we have focused Martin less on revising and editing and more on *rereading*, *reviewing*, and *selecting* pieces from his folder to share with others. Rather than signaling the need to fix what he's done, we've emphasized *reengaging* with it, *shaping* it for others, and *building* on its energy. For

Figure 5.4. Martin's "Trydus" (Edited Text Below)

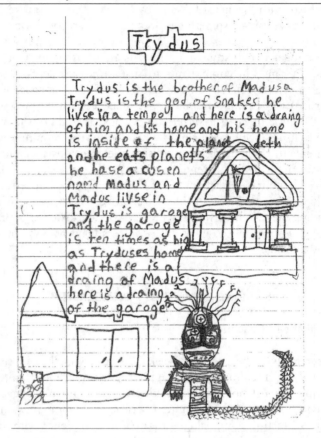

Trydus is the brother of Medusa. Trydus is the god of snakes. He lives in a temple and here is a drawing of him and his home. His home is inside of the planet death, and he eats planets. He has a cousin named Madus, and Madus lives in Trydus's garage, and the garage is ten times as big as Trydus's home, and there is a drawing of Madus. Here is a drawing of his garage.

Martin, representing meaningful worlds symbolically (experimenting with print and communication) and perceiving relationships between text, talk, meaning, and social connection have been major tasks throughout workshop. The collection concept, rather than revision of a single text, reinforces his path and makes his broader accomplishment visible.

Last week, Martin and I talked about how he might organize the collection, and he spent time reviewing his folder and selecting works. We've

Figure 5.5. Martin's Table of Contents

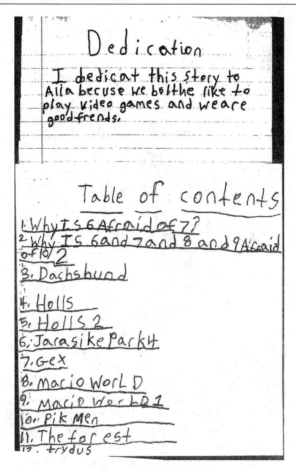

encouraged Martin to create a table of contents, to write an "about this book" foreword, and to compose a dedication page, all of which he's taken up with energy. Today, in our last week of workshop, the collection is complete, though not yet bound. Mr. Allegro invites Martin to come up to share the publication with the class. He comes forward and stands before his peers. Although some students take up this position almost as routine, this is a first for Martin. We all feel it. Students look up, seeing Martin in a new place. Mr. Allegro compliments Martin and says he may have produced our biggest book. Indeed, there are more than 50 pages, and Martin shows us his red and white illustrated cover, with the title: "My Collection of Stories."

With Mr. Allegro's prodding, Martin reads the table of contents (Figure 5.5) to the class. There are 12 pieces listed, starting with "Why is 6 Afraid of 7?"—a joke that Martin has written out in his own words and illustrated

Figure 5.6. Table of Contents for Jarasike Park

in detail. This is followed by a variety of titles. Some are video game "screen shots" (see Chapter 2), others have lengthy written explanations in adult handwriting, others are cartoon block sequences with labels and speech bubbles, and still others, like "Trydus," have Martin's more extended print writing. Most titles involve multiple pages. "Jarasike Park 4," for example, has its very own table of contents (see Figure 5.6).

After Martin reads his titles, I ask if he wants to read his "about this book" page. I am familiar with this foreword, which reads:

> This Book is about all
> sortes of crechers and all
> of these storys cam frome
> a imaginashon frome the arthor
> This book has maps and
> avenchers and exicitment and
> Jokes and Art and gods.

It is a remarkable summary, in my mind, demonstrating that Martin is learning to use alphabetic language purposefully, skillfully, and independently. But Martin simply looks at Mr. Allegro and then says no. Mr. Allegro asks if Martin would like to read his dedication. The dedication, which I have seen, is written like this: "I dedicat this story to Ava becuse we bolthe like to play video games and we are good frends." Martin thinks about this for a moment and again says no. Then we applaud, and Martin goes back with a parent volunteer to put special clips in the book to hold it together. The normal binding process won't work because of the sheer number of pages. The volunteer tells me later that Martin came over to her after workshop and said, "My hands were shaking" and "I'm glad that's over." She says she just told him, "It's a great day for you, Martin." She says Martin said a few times: "I'm just so proud of myself."

Vanni's Writing Is Taken Seriously

June 6, Year 1: I've been working in the hallway with students and get back into the classroom just in time for sharing. Carla's telephone dialogue (see Chapter 4) is ready to share. She and her acting partners, Missy and Ellen, want to go first. Mr. Allegro is getting the class to come together. There is lots of activity, things are noisy, and this takes work. With a teacher voice, Mr. Allegro says, "OKAY, EVERYBODY FOCUSING. . . . Can we pick up this paper? Okay. . . . I'm waiting for Trace to close his book (Trace is reading a "Garfield" comic book). I'm ready for Mr. Cleaners. . . . I'm ready for Mr. Stevens to watch. Mr. Neil!" With effort, Mr. Allegro gets all eyes up front.

The girls perform Carla's eavesdropping dialogue—all their lines are memorized and the acting is engaging—especially when Ellen says, "But I'm big, too!" When they are done, Mr. Allegro extends and builds connections: "How many have had that experience—had someone eavesdrop on you?" Many hands raise, over half the class. We all look at one another. Then Mr. Allegro asks, "How many of you have *been* the eavesdropper?" Smiles emerge, and there's a buzz through the room. Almost all students' hands are up. Mr. Allegro talks about very old telephones that had "party lines" where you could hear other callers. Carla's project is a success.

Mr. Allegro next invites Vanni to share a new publication: "Flying with Snoopy." After several days of keyboarding, Vanni has finished a second story, following on the success of "The Three Little Cats." There are six chapters, ranging from two lines to seven lines of typed text each. An iconic picture of Snoopy, taken from the Internet, is on the cover. The act of typing has taken ages, but as an English language learner, using the computer seems to have benefits for Vanni, both in terms of his engagement with written language and in terms of his familiarity with technology.

As Vanni heads to the front, Mr. Allegro puts his hands around his eyes to simulate goggles: "Everybody put on your Snoopy flying goggles!" Vanni stands in front and holds his book. He says he doesn't want to read anything, so Mr. Allegro just has him hold the book up high so everyone can see. Then a classmate asks Vanni to read Chapter 1. Vanni wavers, but then agrees after someone says, "It's short!" Vanni reads Chapter 1 aloud:

> "One day Peanut was at school. He opened his lunchbox. Snoopy came out. The company made it magic."

Vanni pauses as he ends the brief chapter. Then he goes on:

> "Chapter 2. Snoopy had an airplane and took Peanut to the mall. While they were flying they saw their friends on the playground, their home, and the mall."

Chapter 2 ends here. Vanni pauses as if to finish, but then says he'd like to read his dedication. He is on a roll.

> "I dedicate this story to Martin because he is my best friend. He like my last story called 'The Three Little Cats.'"

Applause follows. As Vanni returns to his seat, I hear a student asking Vanni, "What kind of airplane is it?"

Much has happened in these moments. The language of "Flying with Snoopy" is fairly basic. Yet through publishing and sharing, Vanni's writing is integrated with purposeful social interaction. He is publicly recognized for a writing accomplishment, is actively invited by classmates to read aloud, uses his writing to validate a friendship, and receives a spontaneous content-oriented question from a peer. Vanni's writing, in short, is taken seriously. It has tangible effects in the room. This is significant for a student who, given different premises, might otherwise experience writing as an exercise in discomfort and vulnerability or who might simply be segregated from classmates altogether during reading and writing time.

Acceptance in the Public Sphere

These moments, near the end of our first workshop year, illustrate the influence of publishing and sharing on writer identity, value, and community membership. Publishing events, grounded in participation, play, and exploration, rather than predetermined outcomes, allow Martin and Vanni to experience value in a writing community, to be seen and heard as literate individuals with something to offer, rather than as merely deficient. This is particularly important as both students are working at the forward edge of their language development. The power of public sharing is captured in the intensity of Martin's emotions. Simply standing before the group with his writing, being regarded in a new way, takes risk, courage, and composure. Vanni, likewise, takes up a new position in the room, one where peers now ask to hear his writing and where Vanni uses developing skills to entertain the group and to publicly mark his friendship with Martin. Both students are hesitant about how much they share, yet acceptance in the public sphere is, in a word, transformative. It confers worth, motivation, and membership.

Flexibility in our notion of publishing and sharing has been essential—that is, keeping ourselves open to what "accomplished" forms of writing might be for different students. This allows Martin to bring forth a "collection" as an impressive literacy outcome. It allows Carla to present a play, like Hope's, where she activates social connections and gets to witness her "eavesdropper" theme striking a nerve among peers. Flexibility creates space for Vanni to present a work that fits his interests and needs. Though "The Three Little Cats," his first work, essentially replicated the plot of the classic fable "The Three Little Pigs," "Flying with Snoopy" attempts an original storyline. In his new story, Vanni tries out complex sentence structures, such as "While they were flying," which were not present in his earlier writing.

In constructing public spaces, we form the shape of a community. We generate not only space for feedback but for visibility, purpose, and value. To what extent is there space for all students to bring creative communicative resources into the public realm? Genishi (2016), in this respect, emphasizes the importance of "flex" in educational reform, imagining "a curriculum spacious enough for multiple modes of child improvisation," where students' "fluid choices of expressive modes and their developing identities would be valorized in sanctioned and unsanctioned moments" (p. 161). For students like Martin and Vanni, who may not meet standardized benchmarks, a spacious curriculum matters, one where publishing and sharing become tools for participation, for experiencing community membership, and for the emergence of new languages and identities.

SETTING NEW CONDITIONS FOR LANGUAGE DEVELOPMENT

Sharing and publishing were dynamic, cooperative events that held significant power in our workshop. Public space generated language initiatives—play performances from Hope and Carla, Mary's reevaluation of "Nanina," Vanni's reading aloud at the display shelf, and the very idea of Martin's "collection." Opportunities to make writing public entangled with literacy desiring, with social motivations, language development, and concrete materials, drawing students back into their writing again and again as they anticipated peer reception. Yet, public space must also be seen in its riskiness and in the ways that students at times manage vulnerability to attain what they need. Ava shows great cautiousness around sharing time. Martin experiences intense emotions as he stands before the class. Mr. Allegro and I are aware that the publication shelf itself might backfire, generating a sense of exclusion and failure for some. Amid such risks, students like Ava and Brendan demonstrate agency and creativity in gaining access to what a public space might offer—a chance to have one's writing voice heard aloud or the experience of recognition and validation. A workshop premised on experimentation, participation, and becoming has allowed space for such students to negotiate public moments, managing vulnerability, language learning, and recognition on their own terms.

Sharing and publishing, in the end, played a transformative role in shaping classroom membership. Vanni's and Martin's publishing moments push back against deficit assumptions, offering these learners new and "possible" identities. This is not an automatic outcome of a public forum, which might easily reinforce existing status positions. Yet, flexing our assumptions and commitments, making space for learning as "participation" and writing as "play and exploration," sets new conditions for language development and membership. Martin and Vanni locate learning zones that fit their needs. They enact "legitimate peripheral participation" (Lave & Wenger, 1991), observing, monitoring, and soaking in public uses of writing around them as they proceed. Indeed, over time, both students enter the public forum in ways that seem to enhance motivation and identity: Vanni is taken seriously as a writer by peers, and Martin feels proud of himself as he shares new literacy accomplishments in the classroom.

Such events reveal the ways in which teachers might add new dimensions and possibilities to students' writing experiences. They also make visible the room that teachers have to shape what is valued within a literacy environment. To ask Martin not to "revise" or "fix" his work, but to "reread, review, and select" is a break with a typical "writing process" expectation—and yet, such a decision fit his desiring and led to a valuable public moment. Decisions about "who" can share, about "how writing is received" in a public forum, and about what might "count" as a publication—these are locations where teachers determine and confer precious things, such as recognition and validation of students' efforts. Moving beyond the singular criterion of curriculum standards, how might opportunities for sharing writing retain enough "flex" to sponsor writing initiative, allow for negotiation with the public gaze, and confer membership more broadly among our students?

QUESTIONS FOR REFLECTION

- What benefits do you see in having regular sharing and publishing opportunities for writers in upper elementary grades?
- What tensions might exist for you in allowing a wide range of writing practices in the public space of the classroom?
- What adult practices during sharing and publishing opportunities enhance or support literacy desiring?
- What relationship do you see between classroom membership and language growth?
- How might new literacies and expanded conceptions of writing—digital, virtual, video, online, or other 3-D possibilities—shape public spaces (acts of sharing and publishing) differently from the way they are construed in this chapter?

CHAPTER 6

Shaping the Writing Curriculum Together

This chapter explores the role of a flexible workshop environment in activating public conversation in the classroom. By public conversation, I mean interactions that came under the purview of the entire class and around which some kind of open, shared discussion about writing emerged. Certainly, the bulk of writers' workshop entailed decentralized action—that is, students developing their own writing initiatives, working with partners, moving about, reading and interacting with materials, and conferencing with one another and with adults. A great deal of talk occurred informally. Yet at times, either in minilessons or during sharing time, and occasionally mid-workshop, we would stop to engage some text or question together, publicly. In these events, a particular communicative issue, concept, or piece of writing would become the focal point around which dialogue would emerge.

Dialogue is relatively rare in school settings, at least by some definitions. According to Nystrand (1997), communication between teachers and students tends to remain "monologic"—the end goal being the successful acquisition of a pre-established framework, standard, or skill set (see also Cazden, 2001). This is true even in classrooms where students work actively in small-group settings. Occasions of dialogue, by contrast, require a shift in the positioning of teacher expertise and in our conceptions of learning—from teachers "conveying" reliable skills and students "mastering" concepts to the "collaborative co-construction of understandings" (Nystrand, 1997, p. 7; see also Nichols & Hazzard, 1993). Here learning involves a "reciprocity of roles" (Nystrand, p. 10), where teachers become learners as well as guides, and where students contribute expertise. "Unfolding understandings" (p. 2) emerge through democratic talk and co-constructed thinking, where concepts, materials, stances, and genres themselves are contested and explored.

Public conversation did not always or automatically occur in workshop. Students sometimes simply watched or listened during minilessons as Mr. Allegro modeled how to do something. Sharing time, which came at the end of nearly every session I attended, often involved abbreviated exchanges. Just getting up in front of the group was a massive step for some students. Sometimes, time simply didn't allow for extended discussion, even if student writing had raised significant issues. Yet, when dialogic moments did emerge, unplanned as they often were, energy and investment were noticeable, especially as public talk intersected with self-driven writing initiatives. Nystrand (1997), in this respect, argues that "depth of understanding involves elaboration of the learner's, not the teacher's, interpretive framework" (p. 22). In other words, dialogic engagement that promotes "depth" locates and unfolds *students'* starting points, rather than our own. In many ways, this captures a primary assertion in the scenes that follow—that public dialogue, where elaboration of the learner's framework can occur, is fostered and enabled in a context where writing choice, experimentation, and flexibility are central.

Below, I describe two conversational events that emerged, unplanned, in different workshop years. In the first, I describe an impromptu minilesson where students used self-driven writing experiences to reshape a traditional academic concept. In the second, I reflect on a discussion of censorship that emerged after a student publicly shared writing with mature content. Such conversations highlight both possibility and challenge for upper elementary writers, and for adults, as we worked on shaping a community with reciprocal roles, democratic talk, and "permeable" (Dyson, 1993) notions of the curriculum—that is, curriculum open to, and fed by, the shaping forces and initiatives of students. The emphasis here is not simply to allow expression for kids, nor conversely to shape writing conformity in the group, but rather to activate "mutually expansive interplay" (Dyson, 2013) between the daily practices of children and official curricular expectations.

REVISITING PLOT: TALKING ABOUT LINES AND MOUNTAINS

February 9, Year 5: As I enter the class today, Mr. Allegro prompts students to tell me what they have been working on in their reading curriculum that relates to our writers' workshop. A few students give answers that aren't quite what Mr. Allegro had in mind. He is direct but kind each time: "No, that's not it." Finally, David says, "How stories have a rising action and climax?" Mr. Allegro says, "YES." He mentions how this part of the reading curriculum applies to those who are writing stories, as they try to construct a plot.

The concept of plot becomes an impromptu minilesson, as I ask students if what they are talking about is represented by a line that starts flat and low but goes up gradually. As I say this, I draw such a line on the whiteboard, and several say yes.

"So this is the rising action?" I ask.

"Yes," several kids respond.

Figure 6.1. My Rising/Falling Action Diagram

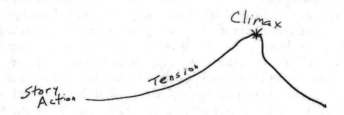

"And rising action usually means there's a kind of problem that is occurring or some tension that is happening. Right?" I talk as I write the word *tension* next to the upward-curving line. I hadn't planned on having a theory conversation today. I'm curious where this will go. I do, however, try to make a few connections. I mention Adam's story, which I have read recently, saying that, in his story, when the evil monsters threaten the world, then that is the tension or rising action. I stop at a high point on the line and ask what that is.

A few call out, "The climax!"

Mr. Allegro asks, "And what does that mean?"

One student says, "When the problem is solved."

I say yes, but modify the answer a bit: "The climax is when the tension is broken somehow—something happens to resolve the tension, and that leads to some solution and the ending." I again mention Adam's story and say that when the superhero group battles with the evil characters, that's the climax. A parent volunteer is nodding her head. Then I draw a downward-sloping line and call this the "falling action" that leads to the conclusion of the story (Figure 6.1).

Then, drawing a separate, single, straight, flat line across the board, I say: "So, good stories usually don't look like this." Students look at the flat line for a moment. I say, "A story like this moves forward, but it might be boring, because no tension or problem is developed. This story," I say, pointing to the flat line, "would just be maybe a series of events, but nothing interesting happens; no tension or action develops." Mr. Allegro asks the group, "How many of you have written a story like that—this happened, then this happened, and it just goes on and on?" At least half the students raise a hand.

Could a Story Be Like This?

Sabina slowly puts her hand up with a question. Looking at my rising action diagram, she asks, "What if your story goes up and then down, and then up and then down? It doesn't just go up and down once?"

I say, "That's interesting. What do the rest of you think?"

Figure 6.2. Sabina's Plot Line

A few say "yes"—as if to agree with Sabina's possibility—but others are quiet. I ask Sabina if she wants to write her idea on the board so we can see it, but she's way at the back of the room and declines, so I draw a series of mountains, like a sine wave (Figure 6.2), and ask Sabina if this is what she means. She says yes. I write her name, "Sabina," next to the line.

I ask again, "What do you all think?" More hands go up. Jason, rather than answering, says, "What if the line goes up and then back down *just a little*, and back up again?" I ask him if he wants to write his idea on the board. Jason walks to the front. I write his name on the board and give him a blue marker. Next to his name, he draws a flat line (Figure 6.3), then a single upward slanted line that then curves downward but then starts back up and then down again.

We all watch, and then I ask, "What do you think about this one? Could a story be like this?"

Several students say yes.

I ask Jason, "What is happening right here?" I point to the downward and upward turns in the climax curve. He explains a concrete plot point.

"Both Sabina's and Jason's ideas are interesting," I say.

More hands go up. Rodney says he has an idea, and I invite him forward, writing his name on the board and handing him a marker. He talks as he draws: "I start with a big mountain, because first I tell everyone what's going to happen, then I start the story, and there's a shipwreck . . . and then . . . the big climax comes later." His plot line has four rising points of different heights (Figure 6.4). I help Rodney stand so he's not blocking his own picture. He has a sophisticated line and is very intent, as if thinking through the plot in his head as he goes.

I say, "So maybe these pictures are showing us that the usual model of a plot is just a *general model*." I point to the original diagram I had drawn.

Figure 6.3. Jason's Plot Line

Figure 6.4. Rodney's Plot Line

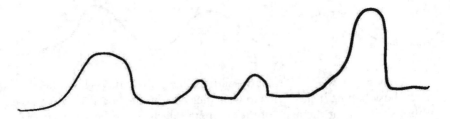

"But actually," I continue, alluding to the student-generated lines now on the board, "there might be lots of ways to create tension and solutions." More hands go up.

"What's your idea, Alberto?" Alberto finds board space and writes his own name, then draws next to it. He starts flat, then has a sharp upturn, followed by a sharp downturn, then a big upturn, followed by a brief resolution, then a big climax, and finally a long falling action line (Figure 6.5).

I ask, "What's happening at the first line that goes up (the brief rising action)?" and Alberto says that this is just the beginning part he's working on now— "the real climax" comes later.

Students are attending carefully to each demonstration. David has his hand up. The main board is full, so Mr. Allegro erases a board to the side, and David draws there. We ask him to use a big voice because he's farther away. Mr. Allegro asks him to use his "giant voice"—noting for my benefit that David is playing "the Giant" in the school play, *Jack and the Beanstalk*. David's line has a low mound at first, then continues on mostly straight with a few bumps, and then there is a sudden, enormously rising line and climax at the end (Figure 6.6). A few of us say, "Wow, what happens there?" David keeps this a secret. "It's something big," he says.

The discussion is driven by students' own plot ideas. In other words, their constructions around plot hinge on investments they have in already-initiated compositions, on what they *bring to* the concept rather than having followed a general formula first. Sabina makes the initial leap

Figure 6.5. Alberto's Plot Line

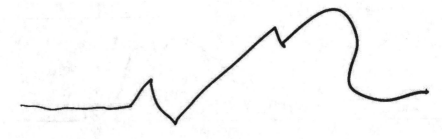

Figure 6.6. David's Plot Line

from the abstract model to her own plot, when she ventures, "What if your story . . . doesn't just go up and down once?" Several students then draw similar comparisons, building on Sabina's initial variation. Their own investments in hand, 4th-graders manipulate an abstract conception of plot and build off one another's representations.

Tina has her hand up, and I say this will be the last comment. She says, "I was going to say, can we start workshop now?" Tolerance for the theoretical discussion, for some students, is at an end.

Workshop begins, and students engage with energy, writing and conferencing independently, and reading stories to one another. I sit at a desk and begin to record the student plot graphs from the board. Two girls behind me confer intently about their writing. Tina and Irene are doing the same in front of me, conferencing on their own without teacher direction.

Soon Tommy comes up to me. He says, "I was wondering, now that we were talking about lines and mountains, if I could write a line to show what's happening in my story."

I respond, "Do you want to write a line like those on the board—one that fits your story?"

"Yes," he says, "because something happens at the beginning . . ."

"Great idea," I say. "Where do you want to write it?"

Tommy says, "I'll just write it at the bottom of the first page." He proceeds to draw a plot line on the first page of his story, underneath his lines of text, as if creating a road map of action for readers—and perhaps for himself.

After I finish my notes, I walk around. Rodney shows me a white sheet of paper with his story now graphed out on a line of rising and falling action. He has taken his plot line from the board and rewritten it for himself, but this time he has labeled each moment of rising action—for example, "shipwreck," "battle of Waterloo"—as if creating a kind of timeline or story outline that includes each point of intensity in his story. Mr. Allegro lets me know later that a third student has independently done something similar today, visually mapping out a story arc during writing time.

As workshop comes to an end, David takes to the author's chair and shares from his writing. The story has a dramatic, even shocking, ending, just as his plot drawing on the board had suggested. A character is murdered. After David reads, one student says, "That was scary."

David points to his climax curve, still on the board, and says, "Now you know why that was so big."

Reinforcing Writer Agency with the Curriculum

What does this scene reveal about upper elementary writers and their learning potential, agency, and needs? In some ways, the visual mapping remains simple—kids represent their own plot lines according to what they feel are moments of intensity in their stories. Lines curve "up" as something exciting happens, and down if not. (For comparison, see a YouTube video [Comberg, 2010] of author Kurt Vonnegut in 1981, in which he similarly plays with rising and falling action.) As a group, we don't interrogate or question these representations—for example, what differentiates an "exciting" moment from a "climactic" one or what rising and falling action really *means*. Instead, we accept, or simply witness, each attempt—being intrigued by how they differ and by what variation might occur next. The notions of plot, moreover, remain relatively traditional. As varied as the student lines are, they still reflect Western-type, linear narratives. Alternate paradigms for story—those considered "cyclical" or tied less to chronology or causality (Bidell, Hubbard, & Weaver, 1997; Heath, 1983/1996), for instance—are not introduced or discussed.

Yet, the public discussion energizes students. The concept of plot, by itself, is not the magnetizing part. Students take pleasure and gain energy from experimentation: from remapping and reconstructing, from trying out variation, the way a jazz musician might improvise around a theme. Such improvising hinges on students' ongoing, self-driven writing initiatives—that is, from palpable story-worlds, compositions-in-process, writer investments that are already active in their minds and in the classroom. These shape the ground from which the discussion emerges, encouraging students to try out ideas in a shared space and motivating engagement with an otherwise abstract model. Understandings unfold on students' own terms. Students do not "internalize" the abstract notion of plot, but rather "appropriate" and reshape it (Cazden, 2001) as it entangles with other things (their own stories, purposes, talk, and emerging visual representations). The concept of plot itself evolves in the classroom. Indeed, had we taught the idea of "plot line" prior to writing—as a planning strategy, for example—would we have yielded the spontaneous mapping and variation? Would we have enabled or restricted the creativity of students?

Dialogue, in this case, emerges as students place "difference" before the group, as alternative lines are presented on the board. Students offer what we might call visual assertions and counterproposals. No formal arguments are made. Each presenter asks, in effect: "Is this structure okay?" or "What do you think of this?" The discussion, thus, reflects exploratory discourse rather than persuasion or argument (Tannen, 1999)—not a debate, but the pursuit of possibilities. Together, we enact a "reciprocity of roles," which takes intentionality on my part. Rather than answering Sabina's unexpected question, I mirror it back, keeping it alive among the students. I trust that students know things about plot, in their own way, and I am willing to give these ideas weight, to see them incubate. I encourage visual representation, so that students might see, appreciate, and compare diagrams. I resist reinterpretation, assessment, or conclusions—that is, elaborating my own framework or providing an answer. Sabina's question, "What if it just doesn't go up and down once?" remains open.

Students take the discussion forward in their own ways. For some, sharing a plot line is not just about expanding the idea of plot in academic fashion but about showing off the unique contours of one's *own* story. David tantalizes us with what his big final curve "might" mean. He plays with audience expectation, keeping us in suspense about the ending, implicitly marketing the story. Again, social and academic purposes occur together. Other students experiment as the workshop proceeds. Tommy asks permission to imitate what others have done during the discussion, seemingly unsure if this is allowed or perhaps just wanting an audience. He creates his own line, taking the original step of inserting it on the first page of his actual story. The plot line becomes functional and communicative—a text. Rodney re-creates his own visual from the whiteboard on a separate paper, now labeling each high point, adding story detail—an activity, I suspect, that might be useful for others. He develops a tool for stepping back from his writing, for considering narrative movement as a whole. David, during sharing time, makes use of his own plot line on the whiteboard ("Now you know why that was so big"), pointing to the visual to explain the impact of his murder scene, interacting with his audience, and signaling awareness of the intensity of his story action for readers. Students experiment with ways of seeing and representing the shape of their writing. "Lines and mountains" become new, active tools in the classroom, which students take up for a variety of purposes and possibilities.

The point here is twofold. First, public dialogue is fed and enabled by flexible, experimental writing norms, by students' experience in locating "literacy desiring" in the classroom. The concept of plot becomes activated in conjunction with self-directed attempts as students have something accessible and personal to which they can attach an understanding. Such a context provides occasion for authentic questions, those arising from students' own writing, as well as invested ways of responding when questions emerge. Playing with the concept of plot together, in many ways, is an extension of the experimentation already at work in the classroom.

Second, dialogue itself shapes and reinforces writer agency and identity in relationship to the larger, official curriculum. Agency here goes beyond having space and freedom to create individual pieces of writing. Rather, such dialogue promotes and enacts the "permeability" of the curriculum itself generating thinking in community and giving students a role in defining what a story might be. Dialogue in a flexibly designed space challenges the technical rationality that stands behind most notions of curriculum—where students are seen as recipients and where success is defined as reproducing pre-established writing forms. Dialogue, by contrast, leads children and adults toward shared engagement with new composing possibilities. Such recasting of roles, and our shared exploration, led to heightened energy in the classroom and to a sense that we had moved beyond simply "doing school."

NAVIGATING CONTROVERSIAL CONTENT

In the next vignette, I share a public conversation that emerged in workshop based on writing content that adults found concerning. As described above (see especially Chapter 5), students routinely shared work in progress before the class. In some cases, such writing was relatively new or had not been seen by Mr. Allegro or any volunteer. On this day, an individual's writing raised questions of appropriateness. Several adults were present—Mr. Allegro, me, and two parent volunteers. In this case, we found ourselves taking up positions of caution, restraint, and boundary-setting in relation to the otherwise "flexible" norms of our workshop. Norms of agency and choice led into complex issues of censorship, freedom of expression, social values, and audience. Yet, the context also provided opportunity for students and adults to engage such issues together, even if we were unsure of what "success" in such conversations would mean.

April 14: Mr. Allegro starts author's chair at 10:15, rather than the usual 10:30. He wants to give several students a chance to share. He announces, "I want everyone giving the respect and attention you would like if you were up here." He's aware that students often multitask as their peers present work to the class, listening with one ear but also rereading, drawing, or trying to make progress on their own writing at the same time. Indeed, a few students have let me know that one problem with workshop is "how short it is," and one boy recently shared his frustration that just as he's getting into writing, "we have to put it away." My own son also let me know that his writing productivity is affected by "the other things," as he put it, that the class is asked to do during workshop—such as "lots of sharing" and "peer conferencing groups," things he tends to experience as interfering with the time he has simply to write. Everything consumes time, and listening to a peer's work is a distinct choice to be made. As adults, we reiterate the norm of listening and respect, because we believe in the value of such sharing, but this requires ongoing vigilance, as well as flexibility on our part.

Today, Kenny reads a Christmas-related story. Mr. Allegro invites comments. The request yields a few responses: "I liked when you said 'Tiger

Claws.'" "Did you actually jump on your bed?" "Good detail." The comments are somewhat perfunctory, but they also provide an interactive sense of audience, validation around descriptive detail, and questioning. Mr. Allegro asks if students could visualize where Kenny was, and Vicky says, "I imagined that his house was different from what it was."

Vicky herself reads next, starting with the line "I wish I was young again." Several students look up, intrigued, and we settle in for the experience. The narrator has a humorous streak, sarcastically remarking that she was "raised by mice." Vicky shows an illustration. But as things proceed, we realize that the story has mature content. It makes reference to child abuse. There is marital infidelity. She reads aloud: "Her husband had been seeing someone else." A locally infamous mass murderer is mentioned, as well as alcohol and the line "everybody was drunk." Students are listening. A few giggle at the boundary-crossing language. Adults shift nervously in their chairs. Mr. Allegro steps in and tells Vicky, "Okay. Move on. Let's not have that part." But she comes back to drunkenness again, referring to someone with a hangover. Mr. Allegro steps physically closer, asking Vicky to bring her reading to an end, and she soon finishes. Adults in the room glance at one another, concerned with what's been shared. During comments, a student asks, referring to the narrator: "Is she watching a soap opera?"

Vicky says, "Yeah." The story has narrative complexity: The narrator conveys not an immediate personal experience but something she is seeing on television. Students in the audience do not seem particularly shocked and have little else to say.

As the sharing session ends, the adults gather and confer. What should we do? How did this sharing affect the students? What experiences is Vicky having? We talk through the recess break.

Vicky's work reflects other stories that have emerged in our 4th-grade workshop, with topics that touch on social fault lines. Some test out sexual themes: Ronny and Troy's spy/detective story, called "Max Power," begins with Max watching a romantic TV show with his girlfriend. He puts his arm around her, and they are about to kiss when Max's beeper/signal goes off. He rushes off to an emergency. The story is clever, as the boys repurpose a 007-like film sequence, even as it carries a number of gender stereotypes. Like Angel and Isabel's "Valentine" piece, the writing touches on romantic relationships—in this case, insinuating male–female sexual contact, before cutting away at the last second like a 1950s movie.

Cole, alternatively, has shared a "Chicken Man" story from the author's chair a few times, which started off humorously enough with the initial draft but now has turned violent. "Chicken Man" has transformed from a creative story about a hybrid being (a chicken man) into the story of a disenchanted worker who was fired by his boss only to return and exact vengeance. Cole has written at the climax:

"All the sudden he jumped and when he hit the ground sharp blades that looked like fethers (*sic*) killed everybody in the restaurant except for the workers." Then, at the end, "An egg came out of the chicken and a little chicken came out and pecked the boss to death."

Cole did not share these most violent parts with the whole class, but they are written in his notebook. I conveyed my own concern with him directly, saying that what he has written is graphic and disturbing. For his part, Cole was surprised and frankly unbelieving when I suggested that violence like this actually occurs and that such writing might be upsetting. "It's just a story!" he insisted with conviction. We decided together, in the moment, that his story at least needed a "violence warning," but I was left with a larger concern that Mr. Allegro and I must address limits of appropriateness and safety with writing.

Addressing the Ethics of Writing

As recess ends, Mr. Allegro invites the volunteers to stay a few minutes, if possible. He wants to have a short conversation with the class, to share openly the concerns that the adults have just now discussed. This is unprecedented; workshop has never before carried over after recess. Students settle in their seats, and Mr. Allegro initiates the discussion, telling students he wants to revisit something from writers' workshop. He speaks generally about "difficult choices in writing" and having "appropriate themes"— trying to spare Vicky the focus. However, the kids' faces show puzzlement and disconnect. They rustle. The world of recess has intervened; their minds are elsewhere. Mr. Allegro decides to speak more directly. He references our adult responses to Vicky's story from sharing time, saying that the writing had mature content and that we had wondered about what is appropriate to share. His tone is not accusatory; it's more like an observation, opening up a topic and a question. Students sit quietly, taking in the new territory. They don't seem nervous, just curious, wondering where this will go.

Mr. Allegro invites me to join in, and I point out that the last story we heard mentioned things that adults and older kids find controversial, such as drugs, alcohol, and child abuse. I point out that these things happen in real life, and they can also be painful and tragic. I frame the issue as a question: "How do we decide when such very real topics are appropriate for writing, or if they might offend someone? Is it always okay to just write and share 'anything'?" This is what the adults talked about during break, I explain. I attempt an example, referencing our local city newspaper, saying that editors at the paper constantly review the content, worrying about what is appropriate, extreme, mean-spirited, and/or who might be offended. Journalists surely support freedom in writing, I say, but they also don't want to harm anyone or turn off readers.

I'm on delicate ground and fear that I am rationalizing censorship. Thankfully, another parent has arrived who will be a guest speaker after recess. He grasps the lines of conversation and chimes in skillfully, giving examples of his own writing being edited and having sections cut out by supervisors. He talks about the importance of knowing your audience. Some language in student stories, he says, might be "too much" for some people but not for others, and we have to be careful and conscious with how something is shared. Mr. Allegro then refers to the school newspaper itself, posing a question: "What if someone wrote something for the school newspaper that was, like, mean teasing of another student? Would that writing be allowed in the paper? Wouldn't the student or a parent be upset if it was published?"

At this point, Vicky herself jumps into the conversation, seeming to want to alleviate the adult concern. She points out that although she read aloud the child abuse part from her handwritten story, she has already edited that part out of her *typed* version. She does not mention the parts about alcohol and infidelity.

Danni then speaks up, picking up on the school newspaper example, which involved teasing. She asks, "What if you're writing about something mean that happened to you—and YOU thought it was funny?"

Someone follows with: "What if you ask the person if it's *okay* to write about them in that way?"

Another student enters, pointing out that Renee was told a few days ago that some people might not like a certain part of her story. Renee tends to write things that she herself refers to as "disgusting."

I chime in to say that Renee, in fact, decided to create a "Disgusting Warning" with a symbol on her cover page, which at least signaled her awareness of the possible effect her writing might have on others. But another student says that the author of the Harry Potter books might still be upset with one of Renee's stories, titled "Larry Potty and the Prisoner of Portapotty," because Renee has used the author's title (*Harry Potter and the Prisoner of Azkaban*) and "made it kind of gross." Renee, listening, seems to take these comments in stride, still proud of her word play.

The class must move on to the next part of the day. The discussion has been brief but intense for our 4th-grade context. Complex issues have arisen. The ethics of writing are on the table, in ways that we hadn't anticipated. Only a few have spoken directly, but the fact that writing is a powerful social instrument is manifest—to both kids and adults.

Boundary Moments as Openings

Vicky's writing and our adult reactions reveal that writing is not an innocent practice. Real stakes and consequences exist. Writing enlightens but also harms and offends. Students live amid mature inputs and realities, and it is no surprise that such things enter into school-based communication—that in attempting to write, students find themselves managing boundaries of acceptable language use. Especially as writing is made public, issues of safety, free expression, innocence, and identity arise. What should students, in fact, be allowed to say? What kinds of "persons" are shaped through exposure to mature content in school, through writing, reading, and hearing the indecorous? On this day, the force of writing is made particularly visible. Language events trigger one another: Vicky's mature content, shared publicly, activates a spontaneous adult conversation, which leads to a revision in the daily schedule and an unprecedented class discussion. Student writing is controversial, alive, problematic, powerful.

These events, in fact, make rich conditions for dialogue, yet not easily so. Adults have significant roles to play around setting boundaries with language. Limits *are* called for, just as they exist in complex, diverse forms in the "real world" of language use. It is part of the work of educators to clarify what is appropriate (developmentally or otherwise) and acceptable, based on reasonable (though not always crystal clear) judgments within communities. Adults in the room, including Mr. Allegro, are all parents of elementary-age children. Our censoring instincts inexorably emerge: the desire to shelter children from weighted realities, to keep writing experiences and identities safe. We enact middle-class sensibilities, positioning Vicky's writing as a breach or eruption in an otherwise "innocent" community, rather than as reflecting realities woven into our very fabric—perhaps the more honest assessment. A desire for dialogue competes with other impulses to control and shape values directly.

What emerges in the discussion, in fact, is brief and contained. Following Mr. Allegro's school newspaper analogy, a few students enter the fray. Similar to the plot discussion above, they speculate rather than giving conclusions—asking "what if" questions. Danni wonders whether offensive language is harmful in itself, or whether the injury depends on context or reception. What if "YOU" (the recipient of a mean-spirited message) thought it was funny? Another student asks about permission: "What if you ask the person if it's *okay* to write about them in that way?" Both students narrow things down to contained relationships between a writer and a single recipient. The discussion thus shifts slightly from Vicky's mature content, which was not directed toward any particular person. Yet, students raise crucial questions about how language harms: Is it by *what* is said, or about the *intent, reception,* and/or *relationship* between writer and (potentially) offended? The students surface issues about how writing functions in public spaces, especially: How might language impact people beyond the writer's intent or beyond an intended audience member's reaction?

These are complex ethical issues. Simply to have asked such questions, to leave students wondering, seems valuable. In the moment, I am pleased that we have found a balance of setting limits and encouraging open dialogue and exploration. The roles of mature content (infidelity, violence, alcohol), bullying, "potty" humor, and copyright (appropriating an author's work) have all emerged. Students have acknowledged the potential impact of language on others, as well as practical resolutions such as gaining "permission" and using "warning" symbols, each related to actual ways in which adults navigate the power of writing in society. We've experienced language as real-world communication.

Only later do I wonder about some of our choices: Speaking of permission, should we have asked *Vicky's* permission before placing her writing at the center of public discussion? She did not seem upset by the conversation, but she had her writing thrust into the limelight without warning, based on adult perceptions, rather than being given an opportunity to clarify or explain her own motives and purposes. Second, is Vicky actually safe? Is she simply experimenting with mature realities, somewhat ahead of her peers, and in need of reminders around appropriate boundaries, or is she, in fact, vulnerable to immediate forces impacting her well-being? The latter concern grew as a pattern of writing emerged with Vicky—for example, continued references to alcohol. (A few weeks after the discussion above, I heard Vicky say to a partner about her writing: "I'm at the part where I used to write 'vodka.' I'm going to use another drink. What do *you* like to drink?" "Cherry cola," her friend replied. Vicky said, "Okay. I'll go with that.") In this situation, I relied upon Mr. Allegro's sensibilities, his connection to the school counselor, as well as his communication with Vicky's family. Vicky was clearly filtering new forms of social awareness, and processing mature realities through her writing. As adults, we needed to carefully assess Vicky's needs, not reading too little or too much into what she presented to the class in her writing.

Comber (2016) writes that it is "a lifelong project as we work out what we know, what we can say, how we can say it, where and to whom" (p. 119). Upper elementary is a time when the span of student maturity is wide and dynamic. Some students and their parents lean into childhood; some look ahead and engage adult realities; others fluctuate. Adults hold childhood innocence and coming adolescent changes in a provisional balance. Clear boundaries are undoubtedly required. Yet, as I suggest here, writing is a unique and powerful terrain for receiving and engaging controversial content, and upper elementary writers can benefit when adults approach such boundary moments as potential openings, rather than only fearfully or defensively. If we can determine that students are indeed safe, how might we reframe such moments as tentative *questions*—as touching upon norms that are constructed in and through communities—rather than only via dictates? Public dialogue involves uncertainty, yet it also can shape whether students have the opportunity or permission to talk openly about the real forces, and uses of language, in their lives. Whether and how we conduct such dialogue might determine whether Vicky learns simply to erase or sanitize the "real world" from official school spaces, or whether she and her peers come to develop complex, responsive selves as writers in community—maintaining agency, risk-taking, and voice while responsibly negotiating the possible impact of writing on themselves and others.

FORMING PURPOSES IN COMMUNITY

Dewey (1938) wrote long ago about "the importance of the participation of the learner in the formation of the purposes which direct . . . the learning process" (p. 77). He claimed this to be among the soundest of all principles in his beliefs about progressive education. The quote highlights not just "participation" in the classroom, but students' role in the co-creation of *purposes* for learning, at the very essence of the curriculum, where both what and why we learn fuse together. For Dewey, this did not mean that teachers relinquish authority, beliefs, and/or expertise in the classroom, but rather that learning and the growth of democratic persons are enhanced as students experience reciprocity, "intersecting multiple voices," and "unfolding understandings" (Nystrand, 1997) along the way.

Our workshop created a context where students, first, had things to bring to the "formation of purposes" with respect to writing. Students were not simply directed in the curriculum toward preconceived ends. Put another way, things were not so scripted or controlled that nothing new could come forth. Varied plot lines were emergent and unexpected, rooted in students' own inventions and self-directed writing experiences. Mature topics, as discomforting as these were for adults, illuminated important territory for developing 4th-grade students. Such things breathed life into the writing curriculum, offering questions, intensity, invoking real responses, and enacting writing as lived communication.

Public dialogue, second, reinforced the fact that writing is experienced and shaped in communities. Dyson (2013) reminds us that "Composing is not only about producing a text, but also about composing a complex, responsive self in a world made with others" (p. 178). Shared dialogue offered students ways to experience agency collectively and in relation to often taken-for-granted dimensions of the curriculum. Students, in the scenes above, show themselves capable of conversing about complex writing realities as they experience writing on their own terms. They participate, however tentatively, with adults in shaping an ethics of writing. They push back against what the notion of "plot" might mean. Offered dialogic roles in the classroom, students bring resources forward and act as responsible communicators, whose own perceptions and linguistic choices can shape public discourse about writing.

A sense of responsible agency is essential to democratic lives, and its cultivation requires various commitments among adults—a commitment to students as viable meaning-makers, involved in complex social realities; a commitment to questions, not just the assertion of answers; a commitment to dialogue, giving students space at times to hear and respond to a range of subject positions and realities. As Comber (2016) writes, children who "discover what they can do with their semiotic resources . . . are repositioned as active citizens who can participate, and exercise power, in their communities and sometimes beyond" (p. 119). Yet, developing an agency-oriented writer identity, as Comber suggests, is "contingent on the extent to which . . . teachers control or open up the classroom to negotiation" (p. 121). In other words, responsible agency arises when students have opportunity, even if just occasionally, to help shape the very nature of what they are learning.

Trusting what students can do with their own resources, of course, is not simple for adults. As Mr. Allegro and I experienced ourselves, the instinct to control is often strong. Our attempts at dialogue were not unequivocally open. But we did try, at times, to turn assertions, and sometimes our own fears, into questions; to draw on students' own initiatives and starting points; and to invite students to hear and respond to one another in a public forum. As adults, we did not need to forfeit boundaries or our beliefs, but we realized that we did need to seek occasions for public conversation, giving students a voice with big questions, inviting 4th-graders to use their ongoing writing practices to try out new ideas, capacities, and creative understandings to shape the goals of our writing community.

QUESTIONS FOR REFLECTION

- In what ways does writing go beyond written products to involve the composing of "a complex, responsive self" with others?
- What about the conditions of Mr. Allegro's workshop allowed the plot lines discussion to unfold?
- What writing growth is happening, as kids offer different visual representations of plot ("lines and mountains") to one another?
- How would you have responded to Vicky's sharing of controversial content from the author's chair?
- In what ways might teachers support writer agency, even as students approach the boundaries of appropriateness?
- What role and purpose do you see for public dialogue in a writing community?

Developing Children as Writers

At the end of our third year, a volunteer dad thanked Mr. Allegro and me for the workshop experience, saying he felt workshop had "let kids be kids." We thanked him in return, but internally I bristled slightly, worried about the phrase "kids being kids." Had some perceived workshop as a place where academics were abandoned, where kids were simply allowed to roam free and have fun? For me, the learning interactions had been rich and complex —certainly filled with dilemmas, but substantively tied to students' literacy development. Students across a wide range of abilities and confidence seemed to find their footing, to engage actively, to experiment with language purposefully, and to develop new skills. The parent's comment, I knew, was not meant negatively, and upon reflection, I had to admit that this father had articulated something I care about deeply, something central to the work Mr. Allegro and I had undertaken: that kids can still find ways to "be kids" in school, or, more specifically, that they are able to *become literate as kids* rather than simply as prototypes of high school students or adults.

The title of this chapter, "Developing Children as Writers," thus carries two meanings. The first takes the term *developing* as a verb, as we think about ways to "develop" or cultivate children's abilities to write, to help them "become" writers. This meaning suggests the importance of adult guidance, input, and systems of instructional support along the way. We have things to *do* with children to help them write. The second meaning, alternatively, uses the term *developing* as an adjective. This meaning emphasizes that our students are already "developing children" in their own right, and that we must learn to see them "as" emergent writers already. In this sense, we value what children bring to us, where they are coming from, and where they may want to go, rather than perceive only gaps or a lack of skills. I have argued, in the previous chapters, that we must hold both of these meanings in mindful balance. I have also emphasized, or tried to make visible, the import of the second meaning.

Indeed, my primary goal in writing this book has been to represent different ways in which upper elementary students can engage writing practices when given greater space to compose on their own terms. I've tried to name what drew students' energies, what practices and outcomes emerged, and what forms of growth or change occurred. I've identified several tensions we faced from an adult perspective. I've used narrative extensively—first-person stories based on my own observations and interactions in Mr. Allegro's classroom—as a way to make moment-to-moment writing experiences palpable. Narrative, according to Schaafsma and Vinz (2011), "resists simple answers" yet "sheds light on veiled issues that more regularized methods of research overlook" (p. 1). In the stories presented, I've sought to unsettle my own assumptions about writing and writing instruction, using less common metaphors for learning at the upper elementary level: *participation, exploration, play, literacy desiring,* and *dialogue.* I've pushed back on linear conceptions of writing growth, conceiving of learning less from a cognitive stance, where students internalize "concepts" and "skills" as they are directly taught and looking more through a social constructivist lens, viewing learning as it emerges from ongoing shared practices, from students being a "part" of something with others.

Such aims are not capricious or whimsical. For me, they represent a form of advocacy. I advocate for a humanely responsive curriculum, a commitment to, in Lenz Taguchi's (2010) words, "the political aspect of making children's meaning-making visible to the world outside the preschools and schools" (p. 10). With such a stance, we challenge "market models" in education, which overemphasize measurable outcomes viewed from a distant angle (Rose, 2014, p. 68). With such a stance, adults within schools might better describe for others where students' communicative motivations lie, how their writing actions and practices function for them, and what children have to teach us about membership in learning communities. Enhancing our understandings of children as writers—of what they bring—also assists us in providing direction, support, and instructional guidance over time.

BECOMING LITERATE AS KIDS

How might classroom environments allow writing to become relevant to children "as kids"? This question applies as much with upper elementary students as it does in early childhood. The question is also tied to concerns and hopes for real students—like Martin, Ricky, Macie, and Vanni—whose communicative resources and concrete writing efforts may be less recognizable to adults and may not fit the given timelines in school. The question is connected to the numerous writers I observed in Mr. Allegro's classroom who explored language, genre, purposes, relationships, and public space in new ways, sometimes writing with greater energy than we had ever expected. Such learners, I suggest, have the creative means to show us "who they are" as writers and how they might need to proceed to new forms of growth and communication, given a degree of space and a pedagogy of listening. Our students still need various forms of support, leadership, instructional skill, modeling, and feedback. There is certainly still a lot to learn from adults. Yet we have much to learn from students—and this, I suggest, may be the harder task, one at risk of being lost in a time of world-class standards.

Elementary literacy scholars (Boldt, 2009; Comber, 2016; Dyson, 2013, 2016; Genishi & Dyson, 2012; Kuby & Gutshall Rucker, 2016) comment with increasing urgency that our curricular frameworks and literacy policies fail to appreciate the richness and possibility of children's lived literacy. Curricular control around writing instruction is increasing internationally as nations seek to tie language development to global education standards. Citing a study from South Africa, Comber (2016) notes that "the official spaces for children to draw and write (with whom, what, when, and how) close down as they go up the year levels. Writing at school becomes more of an individual and predesigned activity" (p. 129). Vinz (in Schaafsma & Vinz, 2011) suggests that, in terms of curriculum, "the map is often overdrawn for teachers and for students" (p. 14), and that students too often are not able to experiment, take risks, or step into the unknown. Such loss of space for exploration and movement is evident even among our very youngest children (Bassok, Lathem, & Rorem 2016),[1] but it is particularly present in upper elementary.

What such scholars agree upon, and what I reiterate here for upper elementary students, is the need for greater "scope" (Clay, 1998, p. 237) in curricular conceptions of writing. Dyson (2013) notes:

> The more restrictive the curriculum, the more opportunities children have to fail to conform. In contrast, writing events "with scope" allow children to participate in different ways with different resources. Such tasks allow teachers to observe what children attend to and, so informed, to extend their knowledge and know-how. (p. 176)

Scope here involves expanding the field of what might count as writing, not simply as if "anything goes," but rather by attending closely to children themselves. It involves bending our gaze toward kids' evolving communicative practices, their initiatives, relationships, and literacy desiring, especially in an era when the adult gaze is systemically directed elsewhere, toward high-stakes scores and standards. Martin's video game drawings (Chapter 2), Macie's nomadic story practices (Chapter 3), Hal and Jerry's complex writing relationship (Chapter 4), Brendan's bid for public recognition (Chapter 5)—all of these events help us consider the generative practices, entanglements, and desires by which children enter into, and grow, within literate worlds.

A curriculum with flexibility and scope not only increases the means by which students access literate realms in purposeful ways, but also, in

Genishi's (2016) words, allows for "multiple and expanded identities" (p. 159). That is, a flexible workshop environment provides ways for students to try on different ways of *being* in the classroom, to experiment with roles and positions, extending "the life spaces of their permissible selves" (p. 159). The narrative scenes above, for example, reveal identities in transformation. Carla, a new student, creates scripts to entice other 4th-graders to help her perform a play she has written (Chapter 4). Her writing is entangled with becoming a peer and accepted classroom member. Valerie must learn to make space for Gemma's need to be "heard"—beyond just giving "facts"—in their shared nonfiction piece on giant pandas (Chapter 4). Brendan makes subtle moves to secure a moment of validation, assurance that he's been noticed and valued in the classroom (Chapter 5). Martin, sharing his "Collection of Stories" before the entire class (Chapter 5), experiences himself in new ways ("I'm just so proud of myself!"). Vicky tries on and shares mature content, testing out what might be possible to say and share in school (Chapter 6). Identity work certainly happens all the time for upper elementary students, within and beyond classroom spaces. Yet, a flexible workshop space made room for such experimentation, exploration, and play to emerge less separate or hidden from adults and the formal curriculum.

By some measures, our workshop was not especially new or innovative. It reenacted many of the original premises of early workshop pioneers—self-directed writing time and routine sharing opportunities. Some would point out, accurately enough, that our workshop had less "scope" than we imagined, that it was bound by a traditional image of writing as two-dimensional, alphabetic, and print-based. "Textual" communication today commonly involves video, sound, image, movement, color, and various forms of digital remixing (Wohlwend, 2016). Our workshop was also not a panacea. As I have tried to make clear, we faced dilemmas throughout: How much time *should* we give students to complete writing? How much revision should we insist on? How important *is* the final product? I do not offer the specific norms of our workshop as an exclusive standard for writing instruction, because this was not something we aimed for ourselves. Mr. Allegro and I tried on the workshop for a few hours a week, even as students continued to encounter a more traditional curriculum at other times: assigned writing tasks (for example, compare and contrast), tracked reading groups, emphasis on fluency and accuracy. Mr. Allegro did not dismantle or transform the entire literacy curriculum. Our goal was, simply put, to see what we might learn when the terms are shifted, even briefly.

IMPLICATIONS FOR PRACTITIONERS

Enhancing Teacher Expertise:
Appreciating and Building on What Students Bring to Writing

What, then, are the implications of our workshop experience? A first conceptual implication is perhaps simply this: that a writers' workshop approach, at least as much as adopting a new set of classroom procedures such as minilessons or the author's chair, is about taking on new *perspectives* on writing, and on learning itself. It involves shifting definitions of adult expertise in the literacy classroom—not abandoning adult expertise, of course, but tapping into new layers of adult awareness. A practitioner's expertise in facilitating a workshop consists not simply of understanding writing processes or knowing ways to help students build their craft or how to organize classroom space differently. It must include a willingness and capacity, in Kuby and Gutshall Rucker's (2016) words, "to look for what children are chasing after" (p. 36).

Upper elementary students, I argue, need such expertise from us: observational capacities and values that allow us to appreciate and build on, rather than discount, Martin's video game drawings and help us perceive Angel and Isabel's Valentine story not merely as a text to edit and revise but as comprising a variety of events and forces, including emerging gender awareness, a holiday weekend, and peer relationships. Such expertise, I suspect, builds upon what teachers often already know, at least latently, about students. It leverages educators' close-up, day-to-day experience with children, tapping into our daily work as witnesses to students' many engagements, motivations, and actions in classrooms. Facilitating a constructive workshop experience requires setting our sights more clearly on where kids are coming from and where their experimentation might take both them and us.

Such a stance, as I portray throughout this book, often left me humbled. In Mr. Allegro's room, students went in directions I did not anticipate, expect, or understand. It was hard to follow the writing purposes of some students. What humbled me, specifically, was the eventual realization, in many instances, that there was "more" going on in students' writing than I had initially seen. Repositioning expertise requires discipline, checking (though not forfeiting) the impulse to "show how" or "fix" at times, tempering one's confidence in what "should" happen next, and questioning the extent to which our adult aims connect with students' energies and purposes. It takes an assumption, a trust, that kids' writing directions may have unique and important purposes that may serve them well, even if we may not initially perceive where they are going. It requires trying on new lenses, even for just part of a week—lenses that help hold our gaze "in the moment" and allow us to appreciate forms of exploration and play in the classroom. It involves choosing to learn from children.

A significant majority of American educators claim to believe in, and employ, process-oriented writing instruction. Yet great variability exists in how process methods and workshops are conceptualized and operationalized (Lipson, Mosenthal, Daniels, & Woodside-Jiron, 2000; Pritchard & Honeycutt, 2006; Troia, Lin, Cohen, & Monroe, 2011). This is why new "learning perspectives" and "expertise" matter. In some classrooms, workshop reflects a block of time given to students to complete teacher-assigned tasks. The adult provides the genre, topic, and/or endpoints, and the overall framework remains centered on what educational philosopher Phillip Jackson (1986) called "mimesis," the replication or imitation of existing forms. Here, a workshop "model" may not shift the underlying curricular frame or the learning perspectives involved. On the other hand, teachers sometimes swing between ends of a continuum, from direct instruction and *giving* lots of expertise to the opposite, stepping back too far and *giving up* expertise by simply letting children write or watching them write, sometimes to be disappointed by the outcomes.

Workshop, as I experienced it, was not about giving up one's classroom expertise but more about enhancing teacher knowing and expertise. It was learning a new craft as an adult, coming to view children's writing attempts generously and in unexpected ways. This often had a direct benefit to students—for example, building up their writing motivations, helping kids "want" to write further, shaping meaningful communication, supporting relationships, providing enjoyment in the classroom, and helping students experience a vibrant writing identity. Such reenvisioned expertise, as I intend it here, challenges our tendency to see student writing solely as an individual quest to master adult-sanctioned genres, such as "persuasive," "descriptive," or "narrative" writing. A commitment to developing writing skills in these areas, I suggest, must exist in conversation and balance with students' own potential energies, writing initiatives, and possibilities. Such an adult stance, as Lenz Taguchi (2010) says, represents a "softer and widened attentive gaze that includes that which takes place in the spaces in-between" (p. 58) as children approach writing. Such adult openness to new forms of teacher expertise may be the only chance for some upper elementary learners to experience their writing as respected and valued in school settings.

Moving Beyond Linear Applications of Learning Standards

A related implication is the importance of exerting agency in relation to the standards that are so present in our minds and curriculum materials today. How might we move beyond one-directional, linear applications of standards—i.e., from the standard, to the child, to the assessment? To what extent do upper elementary students need adults who employ a flexibly informed, multidirectional engagement with standards? Such teacher agency moves at times from standards to the child, but at other times from children's desiring to standards. Sometimes it might suspend standards entirely, so that we can work with and appreciate a child's complex engagement in the moment, so that the "interests" of the standards are not always in control.

We need ways to advocate for children whose needs, desires, and approaches to writing do not follow prescribed timelines or predetermined structures and processes, yet who have legitimate ways to learn and who benefit precisely from experimenting with purposeful communication. Martin and Ricky's tendency to use visual images to think with text (Chapter 2), Macie's confusing narrative about kitties that touches on epic life themes (Chapter 3), Vanni's attempts to publish and share his writing as a second language learner (Chapter 5)—in all these situations, students gained and responded, precisely, as we spent time trusting, considering, and listening to what they were about "in the moment" rather than only in comparison with a given or imagined standard. With space, choice, and trust, such students also seemed to find pathways and motivation *toward* writing standards, perhaps more than they would have done if we had attempted a linear path to standards, ignoring their starting points.

I do not suggest that learning standards should go away or that they do not serve important purposes. We need, instead, ways to place them in perspective, paying close attention to children's actual rather than merely idealized writing practices. Kuby and Gutshall Rucker (2016) suggest that standards "shouldn't be the starting point or the ending point." Standards are "something to question, to plug into literacy desiring" (p. 195). In other words, teachers must find ways to connect students' self-driven writing practices *with* standards, rather than always steering kids into a standard directly. Much of the student work alluded to in the chapters above, for example, reflects engagement with various Common Core State Standards for writing at the 4th-grade level. Writing standard 4.3 asks students to "write narratives to develop real or imagined experiences or events using effective technique, descriptive details, and clear event sequences" (National Governors Association Center, 2010). This standard looks for writers to "orient the reader by establishing a situation and introducing a narrator and/or characters" and to "organize an event sequence that flows naturally." It asks for use of "concrete words and phrases and sensory details to convey experiences and events precisely." Ricky's cartoon sequence, "Archie the Turtle" (Chapter 3), even though written in an unconventional form and not in paragraphs (though clearly reflecting published children's writing), arguably meets this standard, as Ricky uses both images and words to convey humorous action scenes. With support, Ricky thinks carefully about how much textual detail his audience might need and how well his classmates will be able to make inferences on their own.

Standard 4.5 likewise focuses on using "support from peers and adults" to "develop and strengthen writing as needed by planning, revising, and editing." Most students experienced some version of this in workshop: Martin, Carla, and Ricky (Chapter 2), for example, as they worked with me on their visual texts, and Macie (Chapter 4) as she showed her writing about "Molly and Allie" to a peer and later sought help from me on how to write a summary of her story. Partners like Angel and Isabel (Chapter 3) and Jerry and Hal (Chapter 4) relied on each other, as well as on adults, to strengthen their writing—rereading, sharing, revising, and editing even through complex circumstances and peer relationships. Standard 4.6 looks for students, "with some guidance and support from adults," to "use technology, including the Internet, to produce and publish writing" and "to demonstrate sufficient command of keyboarding skills to type a minimum of one page in a single sitting." Most students in workshop engaged keyboarding and other computerized support to "produce and publish" their writing. Vanni, for example, used a classroom computer extensively to complete his story "Flying with Snoopy" (Chapter 5). (Today, there are increasing opportunities for learners to use new technologies for communication and publication, well beyond what our writers attempted and what we made available.) Standard 4.8 involves gathering "relevant information from print and digital sources." Students must "take notes and categorize information," which is reflected in the work of students such as Valerie and Gemma as they wrote and negotiated their giant panda informational booklet (Chapter 4).

Yet, much of what occurred in workshop also stretched beyond what is found in current standards. For example, the Common Core writing standards may not help us see that some students were working, perhaps primarily, on simply seeing themselves *as* writers, as young people with something to say to others, or that Carla and Jerry were working out new writing skills in complex peer contexts. Carla gained writing confidence, and saw the most purpose in writing, when she could connect her writing tasks to relationship building. Jerry sought to maintain and renew his place in an evolving peer group, using writing to navigate occasional social isolation and borderline bullying. Standards may not help us appreciate how Martin dove into video game worlds in precisely the ways he needed—that is, that meticulously depicted video game "screen shots" were the route to advance his confidence and skills with written language and communication.

My point is that children need teachers and adults who hold both deep understanding of learning standards as well as an agile approach with them, who are willing to move beyond one-dimensional or linear applications of standards, who understand that, given room for exploration and even play with writing, students might show us something new and important about their learning and even discover unexpected ways to fulfill standards. This does not mean that teachers will never aim for a standard directly. Teachers, to be sure, manage multiple forces in deciding what to teach and how (Anderson & Dryden, 2014), including district curriculum, their own beliefs, the practices of teaching colleagues across the hallway, parent expectations, test scores, and more. However, students need us to show agency with standards, not passively following dictates for what is expected, but mediating students' own instincts and personal strengths as we navigate long-term writing goals.

Orienting Our Observations—Using Teachers' Unparalleled Presence

I have argued that upper elementary students need access to flexible and self-directed writing environments, with opportunities for choice, social interaction, and movement, in order to locate and make visible their needs, strengths, and energies as writers. Released from predetermined genres and outcomes, at least at times, students can show themselves to us in new ways. I have called for increased writing opportunities characterized by "flex" (Genishi, 2016), examples of which I have offered in the chapters above. Students benefit from having permission to access their own resources (Dyson, 2016), to have a significant role in determining writing forms, materials, purposes, partners, audiences, and even investment level, making space for emergent energies and unexpected initiatives. This does not mean that anything and everything goes in the writing classroom, that adults have no role in mediating what enters the environment or what is produced, or that a "unit of study" cannot be undertaken. Creating space and scope in a writers' workshop is not an all-or-nothing proposition but rather an occasion for activating adult attention and responsive mediation within structure. Whatever forms of intervention we provide, I argue, should involve space for learning *from* students and being influenced by what we learn from them along the way.

I leave readers with questions that bear on how and where we might place our attention, as we consider writing environments that will best serve and motivate upper elementary writers. The questions below represent prompts intended to orient an adult's observations and listening during workshop. They follow from the conceptual implications above and reflect alternative ways of valuing and perceiving writing in school settings. With these questions, I tap into what I see as teachers' unparalleled presence with children, the fact that educators observe nuanced events and practices among students that others are simply unable to see. Teachers may not always be able to "do" things immediately with such observations—such as change a curriculum, respond as we'd like, stop a testing regime—but the act of witnessing and valuing students' choices, actions, and energies is itself a form of ethical action, reflecting Lenz Taguchi's (2010) "ethics of immanence." It is being present to, noticing, holding, and respecting what children might be about in their communications. I thus encourage teachers and adults who care about writing development to consider the following questions, building upon their already-present practices of observing and cherishing children in classrooms.

Seeking Opportunities

- Where might opportunities for space and choice be possible, given the current structure, constraints, and/or strengths of your existing curriculum?

Respecting What Students Are "Chasing After"

- Given a degree of space and choice, what do you notice kids are drawn to? What seems to be energizing?
- How do new ideas and initiatives seem to arise for students?
- What tools or materials do students choose to interact with? How do they interact with these materials?
- How is writing connected to relational action and social realities? How are writing interests entangled with peers?
- What is happening "in the moment"?

Observing for a Wide Range of Writing Practices

- What informal forms of writing (that is, written communication not assigned or part of the curriculum) do you observe students engaging in?
- What forms of writing and communication do students choose? What uses of writing are purposeful and make sense to them?
- What genres are they already immersed in? Given some flexibility, what nontraditional forms of writing emerge?
- How or when is writing embodied in physical action (movement, play, creating physical products, enactments)?
- How might writing that seems incoherent be serving important purposes?

Attending to Participation and Membership

- How does student participation in a writing environment transform over time (not just "how skilled" is a writer's product)?
- How do students and their writing function in a social context (rather than only "what does the content of the writing mean" or "how technically sound is it")?
- How do students engage with public space, where writing practices are intentionally made visible to others? What do they do with opportunities for sharing and publishing? How do they make their writing visible in less formal ways?
- How might less confident or potentially marginalized students experience full membership in the classroom through their emergent writing practices?
- In what ways are students encouraged to exert agency with the

writing curriculum itself, tacitly or explicitly engaging questions such as "What is writing for?" "How flexible is a certain genre category?" or "How does my writing affect others?"

I encourage teachers to reflect upon their own reactions and feelings even as they pose such questions, to bring to the surface the potential disorientation they might cause. What is it like to seek what children are "chasing after"? What fears or concerns does this engender? What limits might a teacher need to apply given a specific situation? What forms of collegial conversation might be useful in considering such questions in context?

The questions above also function differently from typical learning standards, which emphasize what students are "supposed" to do or achieve, or where they should arrive. The questions above emphasize the *virtual*—what *might* or *could* happen—and are predicated on a flexible writing space, where students are granted opportunities to make choices with their writing and where adults take up positions as listeners. Perhaps one barometer of writing curriculum today is whether we even have room to pose such questions in classrooms.

CLOSING THOUGHTS

I've predicated the material presented in this book on the belief that all teachers benefit from modes of representation that cue us toward new ways of seeing and listening to students, that move beyond curriculum materials, instructional techniques, and/or published learning standards as our only reference points. Coming to the end of this work, I'm reminded that narratives of experience, like the ones I've shared above, are "voyages of interpretation" that involve not only analysis but also the revision of our assumptions, or "unmaking" (Schaafsma & Vinz, 2011, p. 1). Using narrative as a medium for research, being so personally implicated in each story, is precarious and humbling. The limits of one's own perspective are made obvious. Others will not make sense of events in the same way I have. In many ways, I've done something that is at odds with my own training. Rather than a clinically designed study, I've pursued a form of literacy desiring, following an energy more than a prefigured research idea or agenda. I've traced the "affective intensities" that brought me to Mr. Allegro's classroom each week, that shaped my interactions with 4th-graders, and that spurred me to write and learn about these experiences. I've tried to live out and model the revising of my own assumptions—and new ways, at least for me, of seeing and listening to students.

One thing I've learned along the way is simply how much happens in the classroom in remarkably short spans of time—that is, how writing events have density and interconnection with other things. There is usually always "more" to see and experience with students' writing. I do not seek to romanticize writing workshop, nor do I have simple solutions to larger political or systemic forces that may inhibit teachers from expanding writing possibilities. Yet, by experimenting in one site with an open and artful teacher like Mr. Allegro, by making space for what students seem to be "chasing after," and by listening closely, I hope to engage you, my readers, in your own pedagogical growth—that is, with envisioning new ways of serving children and their writing, witnessing and advocating for the rich and unexpected literacy potentials that upper elementary students bring with them into classrooms each day.

Afterword

During the writing of this book, Mr. Allegro and I held several conversations —sitting at a restaurant for lunch, at my dining room table, or at a local coffee shop. We reminisced and reflected on our writers' workshop venture together. In one of our last meetings, before this book went to print, I jotted down notes trying to capture Sam's response to the book as it had turned out. Sam quickly observed that our talking and writing together reflected the informal workshop practices we'd seen among 4th-grade students. I shared my notes with Sam, and he agreed to finalize the language below to offer a closing word:

I had long been looking for an opportunity to do something different with my student writers. I wanted my writing instruction to be something more than assigning topics, putting comments on student papers, and crossing out things that kids had written. I hoped for an approach that could affirm and give students permission to explore their thoughts in the context of *their* worlds. I knew of few other teachers using a choice-driven workshop model, and this scared me a bit. Yet this approach, once we tried it, reinforced my belief that enhancing choice in writing predicates a journey and challenge to students that direct instruction in writing tends to ignore. What we did, as different as it felt, fed into a seemingly natural enthusiasm for discovery that I always see in my students. I've been teaching 4th grade for many years; this age group is always ripe for taking risks and experimenting with newfound skills. The workshop we designed allowed students to experience risk in a safe environment—a kind of "safe risk"—that built motivation. When kids began to ask to stay in at recess to write, I knew something unique was happening! I can't say this would happen everywhere, but it was exciting to see such motivation take root in my students.

When students receive true permission to write, it catches them off guard. It's not the usual school expectation to write to a contrived prompt. Permission sometimes takes a while to sink in but when it does, kids run with it. The experience is deeply validating, allowing students to incorporate their own lives and "beyond-school selves" into the act of writing. Having space to bring their interests, worldviews, and personal experiences into the curriculum fueled development. It gave students more windows through which to see and to draw from. Too often we ask students to master conventional writing forms before they experience confidence and joy with writing. Such confidence during workshop seemed to come when students were allowed to create something that worked for them and made sense to them. I believe that success with conventional forms is aided by such confidence.

The workshop approach shared in this book is not often supported in our current schools. I feel the pressure myself to meet data-driven goals, to fulfill assessments that run in the opposite direction of choice or self-determination. Choice and agency in workshop challenge our current mindset of standards and accountability. If anything, educational reform has moved in such a way that expectations and boundaries have hardened. Such outside expectations often feel stifling to me, and continuing with workshop as we did it seems difficult. I understand why some, perhaps many, teachers will find the flexibility we offered uncomfortable, even undoable. Perhaps that is the point of this book: to help us question, from a student perspective, the current position we find ourselves in.

One of the greatest gifts I could receive as a teacher today is permission to meet children where they are as learners. In addition, the writing approach described here needs time to grow among teachers—it can't be mandated or initiated with "here's the new writing program." It would be best to start with teacher collaboration and conversation about goals for writing, and about what we observe among our students. Such conversations would go beyond buzzwords and test scores. So I look to my district leaders not for the latest new program to try (we have cycled through too many of these already), but for a greater vote of confidence, a charge, and increased trust to go "work your craft" with students. I look for the underlying belief that no matter how they might score on a formal assessment, all of our kids are writers.

—Samuel Allegro

Notes

Introduction

1. By mutual agreement and with his permission, I use Mr. Allegro's actual name in this book. All other names, not including those of members of my own family, are pseudonyms.

Chapter 2

1. Wohlwend (2016) suggests expanded terms for student writers—for example, *videographers*—based upon tools made available to children.

Chapter 3

1. The poststructuralist concepts referred to in this section differ in important ways from sociocultural theory (Kuby & Gutshall Rucker, 2016). I use language like *literacy desiring* provisionally, and in complementary fashion, with sociocultural theory, as both framings challenge predominant practices in elementary school writing instruction.

Chapter 7

1. In the United States, often a guidepost for education policy to developing nations, the percentage of kindergarten teachers who reported using whole class instruction over three hours per day more than doubled from 1998–2010 (Bassok, Lathem, & Rorem, 2016).

References

Altwerger, B. (2005). *Reading for profit: How the bottom line leaves kids behind.* Portsmouth, NH: Heinemann.

Alvermann, D. E. (Ed.). (2004). *Adolescents and literacies in a digital world.* New York, NY: Peter Lang.

Anderson, E. M., & Dryden, L. S. (2014). Fourth grade writing instruction: A case study of three teachers in Title I schools. *Journal of Research Initiatives, 1*(2), Article 4. Retrieved from digitalcommons.uncfsu.edu/jri/vol1/iss2/4.

Attalah, P., & Shade, L. R. (2006). *Mediascapes: New patterns in Canadian communication.* Toronto, Ontario, Canada: Thomson Nelson.

Atwell, N. (1998). *In the middle: New understandings about writing, reading, and learning* (2nd ed.). Portsmouth, NH: Heinemann.

Ayers, W. (1998, Spring). Interview. An unconditional embrace. *Teaching tolerance: A project of the Southern Poverty Law Center, 13.* Retrieved from www.tolerance.org/magazine/number-13-spring-1998/feature/unconditional-embrace.

Bassok, D., Lathem, S., & Rorem, A. (2016). Is kindergarten the new first grade? *AERAOpen, 1*(4), 1–31. doi: 10.1177/2332858415616358

Bereiter, C., & Scardamalia, M. (1987). *The psychology of written composition.* Hillsdale, NJ: Lawrence Erlbaum.

Bidell, T. R., Hubbard, L. J., & Weaver, M. (1997). *Story structure in a sample of African American children: Evidence for a cyclical story schema.* Poster presented at the biennial meeting of the Society for Research in Child Development. Washington, DC.

Blad, E. (2015). Cleveland embraces social emotional learning. *Education Week, 34*(34), 1, 12–13.

Boldt, G. M. (2009). Kyle and the basilisk: Understanding children's writing as play. *Language Arts, 87*(1), 9–17.

Britton, J. (1970). *Language and learning.* London, England: Allen Lane.

Calkins, L. (1994). *The art of teaching writing.* Portsmouth, NH: Heinemann.

Calkins, L. (2010). *Launching an intermediate writing workshop: Getting started with teaching units of study for teaching writing, grades 3–5.* Portsmouth, NH: FirstHand/Heinemann.

Calkins, L., Ehrenworth, M., & Lehman, C. (2012). *Pathways to the common core: Accelerating achievement.* Portsmouth, NH: Heinemann.

Calkins, L., Hartman, A., White, Z., & Units of Study Coauthors. (2003). *The conferring handbook. Units of study for primary writing: A yearlong curriculum.* Portsmouth, NH: Heinemann.

Cazden, C. (2001). *Classroom discourse: The language of teaching and learning.* Portsmouth, NH: Heinemann.

Clay, M. (1975). *What did I write?* Auckland, New Zealand: Heinemann.

Clay, M. (1998). *By different paths to common outcomes.* York, ME: Stenhouse.

Comber, B. (2016). The relevance of composing: Children's spaces for social agency. In A. H. Dyson (Ed.), *Child cultures, schooling, and literacy.* (pp. 119–132). London, England: Routledge.

Comberg, D. (2010, October 3). *Kurt Vonnegut on the shape of stories* [Video file]. Retrieved from www.youtube.com/watch?v=oP3c1h8v2ZQ

Dahlberg, G. (2003). Pedagogy as a loci of an ethics of an encounter. In M. Block, K. Holmlund, I. Moqvist, & T. Popkewitz (Eds.), *Governing children, families and education: Restructuring the welfare state.* (pp. 261–286). New York, NY: Palgrave McMillan.

Dahlberg, G., & Moss, P. (2009). Foreword. In L. M. Olsson, *Movement and experimentation in young children's learning: Deleuze and Guattari in early childhood education* (pp. xiii–xxviii). London, England: Routledge.

Deleuze G., & Guattari, F. (1987). *A thousand plateaus.* (Trans. Brian Massumi). Minneapolis, MN: University of Minnesota Press. (Original work published 1975)

Delpit, L. (1988). The silenced dialogue: Power and pedagogy in educating other people's children. *Harvard Educational Review, 55*(3), 280–298.

Delpit, L. (1995/2006). *Other people's children: Cultural conflict in the classroom.* New York, NY: The New Press.

Dewey, J. (1938). *Experience and education.* New York, NY: Touchstone.

Dyson, A. H. (1993). *The social worlds of children learning to write.* New York, NY: Teachers College Press.

Dyson, A. H. (1997). *Writing superheroes: Contemporary childhood, popular culture, and classroom literacy.* New York, NY: Teachers College Press.

Dyson, A. H. (2003). *The brothers and sisters learn to write: Popular literacies in childhood and school cultures.* New York, NY: Teachers College Press.

Dyson, A. H. (2010). Writing childhoods under construction: Revisioning "copying" in early childhood. *Journal of Early Childhood Literacy, 10*(7), 7–31.

Dyson, A. H. (2013). *ReWriting the basics: Literacy learning in children's cultures.* New York, NY: Teachers College Press.

Dyson, A. H. (Ed.). (2016). *Child cultures, schooling, and literacy: Global perspectives on composing unique lives.* New York, NY: Routledge.

Emig, J. (1983). *The web of meaning: Essays on writing, thinking, learning, and teaching.* Upper Montclair, NJ: Boynton/Cook.

Fletcher, R., & Portalupi, J. (2001). *Writing workshop: The essential guide.* Portsmouth, NH: Heinemann.

Gallas, K. (1992). When the children take the chair: A study of sharing time in a primary classroom. *Language Arts, 69*(3), 172–182.

Gee, J. P. (2001). *Social linguistics and literacies: Ideology in discourses.* (2nd ed.). London, England: Routledge/Falmer.

Genishi, C. (2016). The powers of language: Toward remixing language policy, curricula, and child identities. In A. H. Dyson (Ed.), *Child cultures, schooling, and literacy.* (pp. 149–164). London, England: Routledge.

Genishi, C., & Dyson, A. H. (2012). *Racing to the top: Who's accounting for the children?* Bank Street Occasional Papers, 27. Retrieved from https://www.bankstreet.edu/occasional-paper-series/27/part-ii/whos-accounting-children/

Graves, D. (1983). *Writing: Teachers and children at work.* Portsmouth, NH: Heinemann.

Graves, D., & Hansen, J. (1983). The author's chair. *Language Arts, 60*(2), 176–183.

Handsfield, L. J. (2016). *Literacy theory as practice: Connecting theory and instruction in K–12 classrooms.* New York, NY: Teachers College Press.

Harper, G. (2010). Foreword: On experience. In D. Donnelly (Ed.), *Does the writing workshop still work?* (pp. xv–xx). Bristol, England: Multilingual Matters.

Heath, S. B. (1983/1996). *Ways with words: Language, life, and work in communities and classrooms.* New York, NY, & Cambridge, England: Cambridge University Press.

Hillocks, G. Jr. (1986). *Research on written composition: New directions for teaching.* Urbana, IL: National Council of Teachers of English.

Hillocks, G. Jr. (1995). *Teaching writing as reflective practice.* New York, NY: Teachers College Press.

Hillocks, G. Jr. (2002). *The testing trap: How state writing assessments control learning.* New York, NY: Teachers College Press.

Jackson, P. (1986). *The practice of teaching.* New York, NY: Teachers College Press.

Kaufmann, D. (2001). Organizing and managing the language arts workshop: A matter of motion. *Language Arts, 79*(2), 114–123.

Kuby, C. R., & Gutshall Rucker, T. L. (2015). Everyone has a Neil: Possibilities of literacy desiring in writers' studio. *Language Arts, 92*(5), 314–327.

Kuby, C. R., & Gutshall Rucker, T. (2016). *Go be a writer! Expanding the curricular boundaries of literacy learning with children*. New York, NY: Teachers College Press.

Kuby, C. R., Gutshall Rucker, T., & Kirchhofer, J. M. (2015). Go be a "writer:" Intra-activity with materials, time, and space in literacy learning. *Journal of Early Literacy Research, 15*(3), 394–419.

Lave, J., & Wenger, E. (1991). *Situated learning: Legitimate peripheral participation*. Cambridge, England: Cambridge University Press.

Leander, K., & Boldt, G. (2012). Rereading "A Pedagogy of Multi-literacies": Bodies, texts, and emergence. *Journal of Literacy Research, 45*(1), 22–46.

Lensmire, T. J. (1994). *When children write: Critical re-visions of the writing workshop* (Early Childhood Education Series). New York, NY: Teachers College Press.

Lenz Taguchi, H. (2010). *Going beyond the theory/practice divide in early childhood education*. Jefferson City, MO: Scholastic Teaching Resources.

Li, G. (2008). *Culturally contested literacies: American's "rainbow underclass" and urban schools*. New York, NY: Routledge.

Lipson, M. Y., Mosenthal, J., Daniels, P., & Woodside-Jiron, H. (2000). Process writing in the classrooms of eleven fifth-grade teachers with different orientations to teaching and learning. *Elementary School Journal, 101*, 209–231.

May, T. (2005). *Gilles Deleuze: An introduction*. Cambridge, England: Cambridge University Press.

McCallister, C. A. (2008). "The author's chair" revisited. *Curriculum Inquiry, 38*(4), 455–471. Retrieved from www.jstor.org.ezproxy.ups.edu/stable/25475924?seq=12#page_scan_tab_contents

Meier, D. (2011). *Teaching children to write: Constructing meaning and mastering mechanics*. New York, NY: Teachers College Press.

Mikkelsen, N. (1990). Toward greater equity in literacy education: Storymaking and non-mainstream children. *Language Arts, 67*(6), 556–566.

Milner, H. R. (2010). *Start where you are but don't stay there: Understanding diversity, opportunity gaps, and teaching in today's classrooms*. Cambridge, MA: Harvard University Press.

Moje, E. B., Ciechanowski, K. M., Kramer, K., Ellis, L., Carrillo, R., & Collazo, T. (2004). Working toward third space in content area literacy: An examination of everyday funds of knowledge and discourse. *Reading Research Quarterly, 39*(1), 38–70.

National Governors Association Center for Best Practices, Council of Chief State School Officers. (2010). *Common Core State Standards* (English Language Arts Standards, Writing, Grade 4). Washington, DC: Author. Retrieved from /www.corestandards.org/ELA- Literacy/W/4/

Newkirk, T. (2001). The revolt against realism: The attraction of fiction for young writers. *Elementary School Journal, 101*(4), 465–478.

Nichols, J., & Hazzard S. (1993). *Education as adventure: Lessons from the second grade*. New York, NY: Teachers College Press.

Nieto, S. (2002). *Language, culture, and teaching: Critical perspectives for a new century*. Mahwah, NJ: Lawrence Erlbaum Associates.

Nyberg, D. (1993). *The varnished truth: Truth telling and deceiving in ordinary life*. Chicago, IL: University of Chicago Press.

Nystrand, M. (1997). *Opening dialogue: Understanding the dynamics of language and learning in the English classroom*. New York, NY: Teachers College Press.

Olsson, L. M. (2009). *Movement and experimentation in young children's learning: Deleuze and Guattari in early childhood education*. London, England: Routledge.

Pritchard, R. J., & Honeycutt, R. L. (2006). The process approach to writing instruction: Examining its effectiveness. In C. A. MacArthur, S. Graham, & J. Fitzgerald (Eds.), *Handbook of writing research* (pp. 275–290). New York, NY: Guilford.

Ray, K. W., & Laminack, L. (2001). *The writing workshop: Working through the hard parts (and they're all hard parts)*. Urbana, IL: NCTE.

Rodkin, P. C. (2004). Peer ecologies of aggression and bullying. In D. L. Espelage & S. M. Swearer (Eds.), *Bullying in American schools* (pp. 87–106). Mahwah, NJ: Lawrence Erlbaum Associates.

Rogoff, B. (1994). Developing understanding of the idea of communities of learners. *Mind, Culture, and Activity, 1*(4), 209–229.

Rogoff, B. (1998). Cognition as a collaborative process. In D. Kuhn & R. S. Siegler (Eds.), *Cognition, perception and language* [Vol. 2, *Handbook of Child Psychology* (5th ed.), W. Damon (Ed.)] (pp. 679–744). New York, NY: Wiley.

Rogoff, B. (2003). *The cultural nature of human development*. New York, NY: Oxford University Press.

Rose, M. (2014). *Why school? Reclaiming education for all*. New York, NY: The New Press.

Samway, K. D. (2006). *When English language learners write: Connecting research to practice, K–8*. Portsmouth, NH: Heinemann.

Schaafsma, D., & Vinz, R. (2011). *On narrative inquiry: Approaches to language and literacy research*. New York, NY: Teachers College Press.

Smagorinsky, P. (1996). Responding to writers not writing: A review of *Twelve Readers Reading* by Richard Staub and Ronald F. Lunsford. *Assessing Writing, 3*(2), 211–220.

Smith, P. (2010). Bullying in primary and secondary schools: Psychological and organizational comparisons. In S. R. Jimerson, S. M. Swearer, & D. L. Espelage (Eds.), *Handbook of bullying in schools: An international perspective* (pp. 137–150). New York, NY: Routledge.

Sousanis, N. (2015). *Unflattening*. Cambridge, MA: Harvard University Press.

Suárez-Orozco, C., Casanova, S., Martin, M., Katsiaficas, D., Cuellar, V.,

Smith, N. A., & Dias, S. I. (2015). Toxic rain: Classroom interpersonal micro-aggressions. *Educational Researcher, 44*(3), 151–160.

Tannen, D. (1999). *The argument culture: Stopping America's war on words.* New York, NY: Ballantine Books.

Troia, G. A., Lin, S. C., Cohen, S., & Monroe, B. W. (2011). A year in the writing workshop linking writing instruction practices and teachers' epistemologies and beliefs about writing instruction. *The Elementary School Journal, 112*(1), 155–182.

Van Allsburg, C. (1981). *Jumanji.* New York, NY: Scholastic Book Services.

Van Allsburg, C. (1984). *The mysteries of Harris Burdick.* Boston, MA: Houghton Mifflin.

Vygotsky, L. S. (1978). *Mind in society: The development of higher psychological processes.* Cambridge, MA: Harvard Education Press.

Wilhelm, J., & Smith, M. (2014). *Reading unbound: Why kids need to read what they want—and why we should let them.* New York, NY: Scholastic.

Wohlwend, K. (2011). *Playing their way into literacies: Reading, writing, and belonging in the early childhood classroom.* New York, NY: Teachers College Press.

Wohlwend, K. (2013). *Literacy playshop: New literacies, popular media, and play in the early childhood classroom.* New York, NY: Teachers College Press.

Wohlwend, K. (2016). *From achievement gap to time warp: Methods for disturbing reality.* Presentation at the annual conference of the American Educational Research Association, Washington, DC.

Wohlwend, K., & Peppler, K. (2015). All rigor and no play is no way to improve learning. *Phi Delta Kappan, 96*(8), 22–26.

Index

About the Author

Fred L. Hamel is a professor in the School of Education at the University of Puget Sound, Tacoma, Washington. He specializes in literacy and language arts education.